Ashes
to
Gold

Ashes to Gold

Patti Roberts

with Sherry Andrews

WORD BOOKS
PUBLISHER
WACO, TEXAS

A DIVISION OF
WORD, INCORPORATED

Grateful appreciation is expressed to the *Tulsa Tribune* for permission to use the quotation from the newspaper's March 9, 1979 issue on pp. 19 and 20 of this book.

Library of Congress Cataloging in Publication Data

Roberts, Patti.
  Ashes to gold.

  1. Roberts, Patti. 2. Christian biography—United States. 3. Singers—United States—Biography.
  4. Marriage—Religious aspects—Christianity.
  I. Andrews, Sherry, 1953-   . II. Title.
  BR1725.F613A32   1983   280'.4 [B]   83-10429
  ISBN 0-8499-0346-7

Printed in the United States of America

First Printing, June 1983
Second Printing, August 1983
Third Printing, September 1983
Fourth Printing, October 1983
Fifth Printing, November 1983

*To my mother, Martha Alice Holcombe Reames, a woman who con-*sistently lives her life with courage and dignity.

It was she, pregnant with my brother, who kept faith after receiving a telegram from the U.S. Army stating that for the second time Daddy's plane had been shot down from the air over Austria by the Germans and he was missing. For ten and a half months she held the hope that he was alive, and when the American prisoners of war in Germany were liberated by the British Armed Forces, there stood Daddy, thin and sick, but alive.

It was she who held on, white-knuckled, as Daddy bumped his pickup truck over the rut-filled, muddy roads in the middle of the night on April 28, 1947, cradling me safely in her womb until they reached the small hospital in Durant, Oklahoma.

It was she who bathed and fed and held Daddy the last five years of his life, never complaining, never abusing his manhood, never denting his fierce pride as being fully male.

It was she who wouldn't hear of me running home to Mama during the troubled years of my marriage. And it was she who ran unashamedly to me during my divorce.

It was she who went from being the proud mother of a well-known and successful gospel singer, wife of Richard Roberts and daughter-in-law of Oral Roberts, to being the mother of a woman riddled by controversy, incapacitated by loss, a fugitive of sorts in the religious world.

I saw sorrow in her eyes, but I never saw shame.

I lovingly dedicate this book to my mother.

Beauty to ashes
Ashes to gold
Let love shine through
The story I've told

Contents

Acknowledgments

My special gratitude to Marianne Sitton and Mario Murillo, who both insisted that I write with mercy and grace and the absence of bitterness.

Mario encouraged me toward that end with his prayers and his inspiring sermons on purity and holiness. Marianne, likewise, prayed for me and constantly urged me to walk softly and to refuse the seductive spirit of revenge.

I also have a whole heartful of thanks that goes to my Thursday night prayer group.

PATTI ROBERTS

The following people deserve to be mentioned for their contributions to this book. I owe them a debt of gratitude I will never be fully able to repay:

My mother, whose consistent prayers and belief in me have given me the faith to pursue my dreams.

Jean Nydegger, without whose prayers, encouragement, financial support, and typing skills I would never have been able to participate in the writing of this book.

Judy Young and Judy Russ, whose wise counsel and prayers gave me courage to begin.

My Monday night prayer group, whose love and support sustained me during the dark days of last summer.

SHERRY ANDREWS

Preface

March 15, 1983

It has been just over two years to the day that Sherry and I began writing this book. I met her at a concert in Houston, Texas, on February 14, 1981, where she had been sent to interview me for a magazine article. She heard me sing and speak and later told me that I should write a book. I said, "Yes . . . I'd like to. . . . Would you help me?" It sounded quite simple, and indeed she and I thought it would be.

Sherry came to Franklin to begin the writing (or rather to begin the talking into the tape recorder) on March 25, 1981. On her first visit our talks about the years between 1968 and 1979, when I was married to Richard Roberts, were lofty, generous, and orderly. I recalled events and spoke of all the characters in these chapters rather magnanimously. Sherry bought it (or so I thought). Yes, this was going to be one of those "untouched, unscarred, and unscathed by disaster" books. I was looking very much like an emotional giant riding high above the effects of the storm, my heart miraculously bearing no permanent pockmarks of pain.

After her return to her home in Orlando, Florida, she called, saying something to the effect that if it was all so gloriously wonderful between the principal characters of my marriage and me, why was I now living with my two children in Franklin, Tennessee, while Richard lived with his current wife six hundred miles to the west of us—not only another state but, as far as communication was concerned, another planet?

I was somewhere floating between the placid-denial stage and the coming-to-grips-with-reality stage of inner healing. However, Sherry's intense questions began tearing at the heavy drapes that surrounded the inner memory courts. By the time she came to Franklin for our next working session I was well into my rage stage. Hour after hour, day after day, I spewed hurt, bitterness and hatred. The sweet, magnanimous Patti Roberts had melted into a puddle of raw anger. I screamed for justice again and again as I rolled the sins of the camp out before her like a never-ending carpet. I disassembled myself, Richard, Oral, and Evelyn with icy, methodically calculated precision. We all lay in pieces—as did the ministry—as did the dream that had captured our hearts in the first place. Such unleashing was like ripping a dirty bandage off of a festering wound. The sensation left a nauseating taste in my mouth.

I could not weep for my own sins or theirs or anybody's. My heart felt hard, so like stone—yet it ached as it never had before.

Sherry left Franklin with a suitcase full of bitterness and an injured heart. She had hoped to write of faith, love, and mercy, but in the recounting of events neither she nor I could find them.

When she left, it was as if she had taken all of my clothes with her because I felt shamefully naked. In telling the story, all I had told on was myself. All the sins of hatred that I had hidden from myself were now glaringly visible. We were both in despair because we felt we'd been clearly instructed by the Holy Spirit to write a book that would "prepare the way of the Lord" for healing in similarly bruised people. Yet, my memories and perceptions of the past could not be bent to accommodate this edict. I, by my own commitment to Sherry, had backed myself into a corner from which there was only one exit.

I had to get healed!

So, in the space of a few months I went from being a woman who appeared to have a compassionate nature conferring a counterfeit grace upon those who had hurt me and upon myself for those whom I had hurt, to an acid-spewing volcano with blood on my hands and in my eyes. Then I became a whimpering victim looking for converts. Finally, I suppose God had heard enough, because He lifted a mirror up to my face. Arguments vanished and were replaced by groans. "God, help us. God heal us all. We're sick and broken and can't fix ourselves."

In the next few months healing began. The immediate past was where God began His work in me. But He didn't stop there. He walked me backward through the marriage; through my university years; through my teens—all the way back to my early childhood, where He pulled up the roots of fears, prejudices, injuries, and private terrors. It was a drastic and at times an excruciatingly painful process, but the ultimate effects were glorious. The memories of my past were made dear, and the people whom I had hated and feared became love objects to me.

The story that finally emerged from this year of intense therapy by the Holy Spirit is still not a pleasant one. It is primarily a story of failure. It is a story about what happens when well-meaning Christians attempt to circumvent God's plans in preference for their own. It is a horribly graphic illustration of the fact that you cannot evade indefinitely the consequences of failing to obey God's laws.

It is a tale of personal tragedy, but it is more than that. It is a tale that has been repeated with alarming frequency throughout the Body of Christ in recent years. Divorce has become epidemic among Christian leaders. The forces that destroyed my marriage have wreaked havoc in many others and will continue to do so until they are exposed and dealt with in a loving way.

Some may see this book as an attack on the Oral Roberts ministry. It has never been my intention to attack anyone. Because this is *my* story, about how *my* marriage went wrong, it does contain much material about our lives. But the details of our story are neither particularly important nor unique. The problems we faced do not just afflict large television ministries—the pastor of your local church may be grappling with the same agonies right now. There are deadly viruses running rampant in the kingdom today, and they must be halted before more families are torn apart.

That is why I have written this book. As one who has fallen victim to the sickness and survived, I feel compelled to speak out—to issue a warning to those who may still be trying to navigate the sometimes stormy seas of matrimony. Because I believe more strongly than ever in the eternal significance of the marriage covenant, I can no longer remain silent. I believe that the days when Christians can bury their heads in the sand like ostriches, ignoring the problems that are wreaking destruction in the Body, are over. We must be willing to confront sin and then embrace the sinner. If someone had lovingly confronted Richard and me with the sin in our lives and then had pointed the way to wholeness, we might still be married.

Facing the truth about ourselves is never easy and it can sometimes be very painful, but it is only the truth, administered in love, that sets us free and opens us up to the possibility of wholeness.

I hope that by shining the light on some of the dark corners of our lives, both as individuals and as part of the larger Body of Christ, I can in some small way help to set in motion the healing process which I believe is so desperately needed by the Church today.

CHAPTER ONE

Divorce Granted

The *Tulsa Tribune* carried the story on page 3 of its March 9, 1979, edition.

"Patti Roberts seeks divorce," the headline announced. The story that followed was brief and to the point.

"Patti Roberts filed for divorce Thursday from Richard Roberts, son of evangelist and Mrs. Oral Roberts.

"A 'state of incompatibility' was cited as the reason for the divorce. Neither was available for comment Thursday, but an Oral Roberts spokesman said he was 'sorry about the divorce.'

"Mrs. Roberts is seeking custody of the couple's two children, Christine, 8, and Julene, 7. The two were married on November 27, 1968.

"Patti Roberts, a singer, resigned as a regular performer on the Oral Roberts television programs more than two years ago to pursue her own career, according to Ron Smith, chief of staff for the Oral Roberts ministries. The two have been separated about a month, Smith said.

"'We wish there was an easy way to do this, but there's not. We feel bad about the divorce, but if it's done, it's done,' said Smith. 'We really do wish her the best.' Smith added that Richard will remain active in the ministry and on the television programs.

"The petition, filed in Tulsa County District Court,

also seeks equitable property division, alimony, child support and attorney fees.

"Oral Roberts was out of town and unavailable for comment."

Reading it while sipping my first cup of coffee, I reflected with bitterness on the irony of it all. The death of a marriage, ten years of ministry, of shared joys and sorrows and two beautiful children, were all dispatched in seven concise paragraphs, accompanied by a smiling publicity photo of me.

The article was so much like the marriage had been—correct, businesslike, carefully presented to provide the best public face, but concealing a swirling cauldron of pain and anger.

My verdict on the destruction of our family was much harsher. I had delivered it in my diary a month earlier, during the height of the divorce proceedings.

There's no place to begin retelling this tragedy and at the moment there seems to be no place to end the story. After ten long, sad years, Richard and I are getting a divorce. Divorce, how common. How unlike Christian celebrities to have such a human tragedy strike them.

Divorce seems to be a major, rampant epidemic in the U.S., and the dear Christian community is not immune to having the disease strike its own. Only those who have been inoculated with deep abiding respect and love, preventive education, and family building can hope to be saved from the sickness. Unfortunately, we were never vaccinated. And only in the advanced stages of the disease did someone tell us that it must be done. Too late. We'd patterned our lives after spiritual fame and success. A corporate marriage . . . Christian style. And it failed. We knew how to be religious,

*but we knew so little about the graces and pitfalls of
just being human.*

This marriage has been dead for so long all we had was a
polite relationship designed not to upset the flow of dollars
into the prized ministry.

I think we both really tried to be married, to make it work.
There have probably been as many ardent prayers said about
and for this marriage as there have been for anything.

I feel like the sweet backwoods fanatic who, upon hearing of
the death of her child, runs to the little dead baby, throws
herself over the lifeless form and begins praying to God to
restore life. One quotes all the "only believe, all things are
possible" Scriptures and keeps on believing, praying, saying,
"It is not over" to the casual passerby. The child might
appear to be dead, but is only ill or resting. Dead, no, it
couldn't happen.

The poor woman lies down on top of that child till the
fumes of death choke her. The skeleton of what was is all that
lies before her. Finally, in a moment of mercy, she has the
clear understanding that the child has gone forever. She
stands up, past weeping, past public longing. Only she
knows the sorrow of loss and failure of faith all mingled
together.

What can one do but bathe, put on fresh clothing, and go
on toward tomorrow, knowing that God, in His perfect love,
has provided a tomorrow?

I know that millions of lovely people will find justification
in hating me, as if hating me will protect their own worlds
from similar tragedies. I guess they'll never see that I've lived
in the graves, among the dead, where people come to "ooh"
and "ahh" over the beauty of the monument. How lovely are
the markers. It might be a nice place to visit but it is no place
to live and try to raise two beautiful children to have an
understanding of the joys and treasures of real life.

I'm not just divorcing Richard, but a whole realm that puts religious achievement and lifestyle above the sanctity of life. I'm divorcing the end-justifies-the-means theory. I'm divorcing the belief that products are more important than people. I'm divorcing the god of family image. Perhaps no image at all and a torn family are warmer and more sustaining. I'm divorcing the preference for public prayers over private penitence.

I'm divorcing the person who never learned that "a man shall leave his father and mother and the two shall become one." Somehow, the secret of that formula was never unlocked. I'm divorcing the mentality that caused the last act of this marriage to be handled with the publicity value in mind. Oh, dear God, help me to the other side.

Richard and I had first agreed on December 5, 1978, to get a divorce. We decided it would be uncontested and he wanted to get it done as quickly as possible, preferably before the first of the year.

By December 18, I had moved out of our house into a condominium and had hired a lawyer. It was difficult to find one in Tulsa who had not worked for Oral Roberts University and who didn't have anything to lose or gain by handling the case. Finally, with the help of my brother Ron Holcombe, I located a good, honest Catholic man. When I told him Richard wanted the divorce finished by January, he just laughed and said, "Honey, this is not a television program or a publicity event; this is a divorce and we'll get it done when we can. If he's too busy to get a divorce, that's his problem."

So, a few days before Christmas, the lawyers called a meeting and we all gathered in Oral's dressing room at Mabee Center, the main auditorium at Oral Roberts University. Everyone was very uncomfortable. I looked at

Richard's lawyers, the men I had worked with for years, and I couldn't believe we were adversaries now. It grieved us all. I could see the pain in their eyes when they had to say harsh things to me, and I thought, "Oh, I'm so sorry for you. I'm sorry that this is your job!"

At that meeting it was decided that I should file for the divorce. Richard had assumed all along that I would file. When I told him that I wasn't going to, he said, "But you have to. I certainly can't."

So my attorney presented them with a list of conditions they would have to meet if they wanted me to file. If I was going to take the blame publicly they would have to make financial concessions, which they agreed to do without protest. It was all very businesslike. But I didn't realize how completely businesslike everything had become until several weeks later. I had gone back to our home to pack a few clothes. While I was there, Richard came into the bedroom and said, "I'm so sorry our marriage didn't work out," and extended his hand for me to shake. That was why it seemed so odd to me when I read the newspaper account saying that I had sued Richard for divorce. I never thought of myself as *suing* Richard; it was just the way we had all agreed this one had to happen.

I filed on March 8, and my attorney drew up an emergency decree and petitioned the judge to grant a quick decision in order to avoid a lot of unpleasant publicity.

The next day I was scheduled to appear in Judge McLemore's chambers at 2:00 P.M. My brother Ron and my attorney accompanied me. Richard didn't come; his attorneys represented him. The atmosphere in the judge's chambers was very grave. After making our perfunctory hellos, no one said anything until Judge McLemore arrived.

Looking around the darkly paneled office, I noticed along one wall an arrangement of family pictures. Three fresh-faced children laughed out at us. I smiled thinly back at them. They provided the only touch of warmth in the room.

Judge McLemore entered and studied the papers for a few moments. Then he turned to me and said, "You realize that when I sign this decree it's all over? Do you agree to all the terms of the settlement?"

I said, "Yes, I agree."

"After this you can make no further claim to Richard's money or any of his assets, excluding, of course, any special needs that the children might have," he added.

"I understand that," I replied.

"Well, in that case, I don't see any reason not to grant this," he said and signed his name. I signed mine above it. Richard had presigned the document.

The entire ceremony took about fifteen minutes. When it was over the judge said, "Patti, there are reporters downstairs, so I'm going to sneak you out the back elevator."

My secretary, Beverly Hubbard, was waiting for me in the parking lot. She put her arm around me and said, "Hey, are you going to be all right?" I nodded, then said, "Beverly, I'm hungry. Let's go get something to eat."

We went to a little French restaurant down the street. Throughout our lunch I felt sure everybody in the restaurant was staring at me. Tulsa's not that big, and since my picture had been in the paper that morning, news of the divorce had traveled fast. "Beverly, I'm so embarrassed," I said. We ate quickly and left.

I had a concert to sing in Atlanta over the weekend, and Beverly was going with me. We were both looking forward to getting out of town for a few days. But when we arrived at the Tulsa airport we realized that ORU had just let out for spring break and the airport was filled with ORU students. Everywhere I looked, someone was staring at me.

I had just sat down in a chair to wait for a plane when one of them came up, knelt beside me, handed me a note, and walked away. I opened it and read, "We love you and are praying for you and we'll always love you." It was signed simply, "Robin." I began to cry. I looked around and all the students were looking at me. My make-up was running down my face. I called Robin over.

"You'll never know what this means to me," I told her. "You are so kind to say that you still love me."

As it turned out, Robin was also going to Atlanta. When we got off the plane she introduced me to her parents, Rev. Terry Mulford and his wife, Kathy. "Patti just got a divorce today," she told them. Of course, they were shocked, but mercifully they didn't react with horror. They were very solicitous and offered Beverly and me a ride to our hotel.

Normally, I never let anyone take me to my hotel. I'd rather ride a taxi and pay a thousand dollars than go with a stranger. I'm too shy. But I was so disoriented and Robin had been so sweet to me that I accepted Rev. and Mrs. Mulford's offer.

They took us to the Peachtree Plaza and we sat out in the car for an hour while they prayed with me and for me.

Rev. Mulford told me, "God's not finished with you yet." I was thinking, "Sure, I've just divorced Richard Roberts. It's over for me. God's through with me." But they each kept repeating, "No, honey, it's not over. God loves you. God loves your children, and you'll see, He'll watch out for you. He'll take care of you." They just pumped the love of God into me, and I drank it in like thirsty ground in a summer rainstorm. My soul had been parched for so long, I couldn't get enough of their love and acceptance. I kept asking them over and over, "Are you sure God hasn't forgotten me?" and they repeated, "Yes, honey, we're sure. God can fix even this."

As I got out of the car I said to them, "I don't really know you, but you'll never understand how much you've helped me. I appreciate your kindness and encouragement. You've given me comfort and I thank you."

Beverly and I checked into the hotel, and I got in bed and pulled the covers up over my head. I whispered from beneath the sheets, "I don't know how I got through this day, Lord. It's one thing to sneak out of a judge's chambers to avoid the press, but to end up in an airport filled not just with Tulsans but with ORU students and then to have You send someone to protect me and to say, 'I love you,' is just too kind. I don't know why You love me. I don't have a television show or any power to do anything terrific for You, but thank You for watching out for me. I know I've made a mess of my life and I'm sorry I've embarrassed You so much. But if there's anything left of my life that You can use, please take it. Don't give up on me, God—please find a way to use me."

CHAPTER TWO

—Drawn by a Dream—

September 5, 1965, was blazing hot—a perfect Indian summer day. Heat waves shimmered off freshly poured concrete walks while a blistering west wind kicked up a cloud of red dust and sent it dancing through the brilliant blue Oklahoma sky.

Bulldozers belched columns of black smoke and diesel fumes which combined with the swirling dust to bring stinging tears to my eyes. Workers with blueprints in hand scurried across plank walkways shouting directions at crane operators whose machines were stretching their giant necks lazily to the skies.

Oral Roberts University would open its doors to its first class of freshmen in two weeks. Oral's dream of building a university that would send its graduates out as missionaries to every corner of the globe and to every sphere of man's endeavor was coming to life, and I was going to be part of it.

As I stood at the entrance to the University, the shirt of my gray wool suit sticking to my back and covered with a fine blanket of dust, I thought I had never seen anything so beautiful. The moment I stepped on campus I felt the presence of the Lord, and I was so at home in it, I never wanted to leave.

That I should be here at all still seemed like a dream to

me. Certainly there had been little in my background to prepare me for anything like ORU.

I grew up in Tigard, Oregon, a bedroom community of Portland, nestled comfortably in the lush Willamette Valley. I was the middle child and only daughter of Hulitt and Alice Holcombe. I had two brothers, Alan, two years older than I, and Ronald, two years younger.

Oregon's topography has enormous variety, and Tigard is perfectly situated to benefit from it. We were less than three hours away from the beach or the ski slopes and about four hours from the desert, as well as being close to the Canadian border.

Oregon is a green and rainy state with dense forests, hillsides bursting with color, and peaks that never lose their snow. Everywhere I looked there was incredible natural beauty. I could walk a block from my house, climb a hill and view a breathtaking panorama. The Willamette valley spread out before me like a thick green carpet and in the distance stood Mount Hood, looking like a big scoop of vanilla ice cream plunked down in the middle of it.

Next to my house was a whole block of Douglas fir trees, huge trees that an adult couldn't put his arms around. As a child, I would lie in bed at night and listen to the music the wind made as it blew through those trees.

We lived in an unpretentious white frame house on Walnut Street. It had a big yard with very thick grass which was almost always in need of a trim. It was my brothers' responsibility to take care of the yard, and since they hated the task and avoided it as often as they could, in the battle between the lawn and my brothers the lawn always had a slight edge.

In the front of the house there were holly trees and

laurel bushes which were green year round, and down
by the road was a laurel hedge that stood about waist-
high. Many times we would tie a purse on a string, lay it
out in the street, then hide behind the hedge and wait for
people to stop their car and try to pick it up. When they
did, we'd pull the string and jerk the purse back through
the hedge. It's the oldest trick in the book, but we didn't
know that. We thought we were terribly clever.

Our yard and the yard of the Schroeders', who lived
across the street, were gathering places for all the neighborhood kids. By the hour we played softball, hide and
seek, and tag, stopping only when the neighborhood
mothers came out and insisted it was time to come in. I
can still remember the delicious feeling of cold, wet grass
on bare feet.

On warm days we'd go down the hill behind the
Schroeders' house to the creek. Fanno Creek had an old
Indian bridge made out of a hollow log, and we waded in
the murky water to look for arrowheads and crawdads.

In the summer, my brothers and I were always put to
work picking strawberries. Because the Willamette Valley is so fertile and the growing season is so long, agricul-
ture is one of the main industries in Tigard. The town is
ringed by berry farms, and everyone's freezers are always filled with fresh fruits of all descriptions. I spent
many hours helping my mother can green beans,
peaches, pears, apples, and a variety of other fresh vegetables and fruits for the coming winter.

In the fall of each year we went hunting in the pine
forests of eastern Oregon. My father and brothers and I
would often be joined by an assortment of uncles, aunts,
and cousins. We'd take tents and set up camp next to a
stream. The water was always so icy that we'd sink our
milk and other perishables in it.

We'd get up very early when the animals came to water, and hunt for a couple of hours. Then we'd come back to camp, crank up the old Coleman stove, peel and slice potatoes, fry bacon and eggs, and eat until we couldn't hold another bite. Then we'd nap for a few hours and start the whole process over again.

Because fresh game was so plentiful, almost everybody hunted for food. Throughout the fall, during hunting season, the woods would be filled with hunters. By Sunday afternoon there would be long lines of cars, trucks, and campers, snaking their way down the mountainside with deer strapped to their roofs. We'd take the animals to a butcher shop and have them dressed. Then we'd take the hides to a tannery and have work gloves and slippers made out of them.

Throughout the year, we also fished the freshwater streams and rivers. Our freezer was always well stocked with salmon, steelhead, and smelt. Smelt is a small fish about three inches long. We'd cut the heads off, clean them out, and fry them in corn meal and oil. Many nights we had fried smelt and fresh vegetables. We seldom bought anything at the grocery store except bacon and a few essentials like flour and our favorite breakfast cereals. There was always plenty of food, and even the poor people ate well.

Self-sufficiency was very important in Tigard. I didn't know anybody on welfare. The people were high-spirited, hard-working, and very proud. It was a conservative community with solid, middle-class values—the kind of place Norman Rockwell captured with such affection and immortalized on decades of *Saturday Evening Post* covers.

My father was the most important person in my young life. He doted on me as the only girl, a fact that irritated my brothers. They referred to me derisively as "queenie." Like most brothers and sisters, we fought, as they say, "like cats and dogs" among ourselves, but we always presented a united front to outsiders.

Daddy sold wholesale auto parts, and he often had to pay sales calls at the auto parts stores in all the little towns around Portland. Occasionally, as a special treat, he'd take one of us with him. When it was my turn, I felt like Queen for a Day as we bumped along the backroads in his Chrysler, laughing and talking and just enjoying being with each other.

To this day I know exactly what an auto parts store smells like. I know what it's like to walk between rows of shelves where there are gaskets and rubber hoses. I know the smell of grease on ball bearings. In fact, years later, after I had become well known as Patti Roberts, I would walk into an auto parts store and think, "No one here knows that this whole store is me. They think I'm an oddity, but I'm more at home here than they are."

One of those trips stands out particularly in my memory. It was early April, a glorious, sun-washed day with still a hint of chill in the air. The cherry and apple trees were in full bloom and the countryside exploded with the brilliant colors of millions of wildflowers along the roadside. The air hummed and buzzed with the symphony of birds and insects celebrating the arrival of spring.

The first town on our route that day was Multnomah. But instead of heading straight to the auto parts store as he usually did, Daddy pulled up in front of a little dress shop right on the main street. He helped me down from the car, took me inside, and presented me to the salesgirl. "I want the best outfit you have for this little girl," he said.

I couldn't believe my ears. Grandma made most of my clothes and Daddy *never* went shopping.

The saleslady dressed me like a little doll in a green tartan plaid skirt with little tartan suspenders and a white ruffled blouse. Pure white stockings and black patent leather shoes completed the outfit. I had never felt so beautiful.

I was five years old and suffered from amblyopia, an eye disease that caused my left eye to cross until I was about seven. I wore tiny white plastic glasses with gold flecks in them. These were topped off by jagged bangs I had cut myself, using Mama's best kitchen scissors. The total effect must have been rather comical, but Daddy thought I was pretty, and he had just proved it by buying me this outfit. That was the first recollection I have of feeling truly special to Daddy.

It was an especially extravagant gesture on his part because we had very little extra money in those days. I never had more than four or five dresses, but we didn't think of ourselves as poor or disadvantaged.

Daddy was very generous and was always giving money away. If we were down to our last fifty dollars in the bank and a friend asked to borrow it, Daddy would draw it out of our account and give it to him. He also had a soft heart for people in trouble. We took in several boys from broken homes and raised them, and we always had a couple of uncles or grandparents or somebody staying with us. I'm sure Daddy's generosity must have given Mother some sleepless nights, but it taught my brothers and me that it is hard to feel poor when you're giving money away.

Friends and family were very important in Tigard. My relatives came to visit every weekend, or we went to visit them. We always had a houseful of people. Our dinner table was filled with either laughter or controversy. We never had a dull dinner, and to this day I don't know how to eat in silence.

When I was about ten, Mama and Daddy decided that I should take piano lessons. I wasn't too excited about the prospect at first, especially since my lessons were at 9:00 on Saturday morning.

My teacher's name was Mrs. Huddleston, and she lived about twenty miles from our house out in the country. You had to climb the mountains to get to it. I can remember many Saturday mornings leaving our house early when the valley was still thick with fog. As we climbed the mountains the fog would slowly dissipate until we reached the top. There the sun would break through and everything would be illuminated with glorious light, while below us on the other side, the valley was still fogged in. It was a beautiful sight and almost worth the effort of getting up on a Saturday morning to see.

Mrs. Huddleston lived in a large old house which sat right on a river. There was a big wood stove in her kitchen, and in the winter she always had a fire blazing in it. Lessons were conducted in her parlor, on an ebony grand piano. The room was filled with pictures of her students, and there were always a couple of fat, lazy cats curled up on the sofas and chairs.

Mrs. Huddleston, an older woman with beautiful gray hair which she kept curled, was always made up like a china doll, all pink-cheeked and perfumed. She sat beside me in a chair, and sometimes she would play along.

She was an excellent teacher and devoted to her students. Every year she entered them in state competitions and they always won superior marks. She also made her students do recitals regularly. Recitals always terrified me and I hated them, but they did have one saving grace: Mrs. Huddleston would let me make up my own music and perform it as part of my program. She always encouraged creativity in her students, and I am very grateful to her for that. She was one of the few people in my life who encouraged my creative urges.

About the same time that I began taking piano lessons, I also started singing in the church choir. It was there that I realized for the first time that I had a reasonably good voice and that singing was enjoyable.

Church was a focal point of our lives, providing most of our social outlets as well as our spiritual nourishment. We belonged to the Tigard Assembly of God on Greenburg Road. It was a store-front church—a two-story, square stucco building, which didn't have stained glass windows.

Daddy was a founding deacon and a pain in a lot of preachers' necks. He was so opinionated he just drove them crazy—especially if they were Republicans. Daddy was as partisan in his politics as he was in his religion. He was a New Deal Democrat, and woe to the poor preacher who confessed to being a Republican. He earned Daddy's instant contempt. "Roasted preacher" was a fairly frequent item on our Sunday menu. Nevertheless, Daddy loved that church and was one of its most faithful supporters.

Although we were Pentecostals, we were not the "Holy Roller" variety. We were legalistic Pentecostals. Ours was a fundamentalist church, a very closed organization, spiritually elite, and, for the most part, spiritually cold. However, occasionally there were great moves of God, and I can remember, even as a young child, praying at the altar and weeping before God.

Every summer we went to camp meeting. It was always held at Brooks, Oregon, which was twenty or thirty miles south of our house. It had a big old board building with a roof, a hamburger shack, an administration building, and cabins on the grounds where people could stay. I always thought it would be special to stay in one of them but we never did. We always drove down, day after day.

My brothers and I disliked camp meeting. During the day Mother and Daddy would go off to services and we'd go to the playground, but we all had to attend the evening services. I spent many hours dangling my feet in the sawdust while numerous people talked about things in which I had yet to develop an interest.

My parents reinforced the lessons of church at home. Every night Mama would pray for us before we went to bed and many evenings after she had tucked us in, she would go into the living room and practice hymns on our upright piano. Mama never had piano lessons and she only knew how to play on the black keys and only in intervals of open fourths and fifths, so all the great hymns of the church sounded Chinese. But that never dampened her enthusiasm. She'd pound furiously away at that old piano for hours.

Many nights I'd lie in bed and have wet-eyed talks with the Lord while she played her Chinese version of "Amazing Grace." I'd close my eyes and imagine Jesus sitting in the little white rocker beside my bed, and I'd whisper to Him, "Oh, Jesus, I love you so much. Please use me . . . please use me. . . . Whatever happens in my life, just let me be your friend. I don't care what You want to do with me. Just use me for something."

And I believe that in spite of my errors in life, He's honored that because as a child I asked Him with a pure heart and that desire has stayed with me all my life. My

failures have not been able to extinguish it, nor my rebellion nor my disappointments nor my conflicts with
other people or myself.

In spite of my desire to be used by God, I never
dreamed of being a singer or what some people would
call a "Christian celebrity." Those thoughts never even
entered my mind. Women in Tigard didn't have careers
or ministries. They were wives and mothers and, occasionally, teachers. It never occurred to me that things
could or should be any other way. My horizons were as
limited as if they had actually been marked off at the
town's boundaries.

But when I was fifteen, an event occurred that began to
open the windows of my soul to the world beyond Tigard. A girl friend of mine, Sherry Meier, read in the
newspaper that a Christian musical group called the
Continentals was holding auditions in Portland and was
looking for high school students who could sing. I had
sung in the church choir for years but I never considered
myself particularly talented. Under Sherry's urging,
however, I auditioned, and, to my great surprise, was
selected.

The Continentals, who were sponsored by Youth for
Christ, sang every Saturday night during the school year
at YFC meetings in Portland. In the summer we went on
tour. We'd pack onto a little semi-air-conditioned bus
and travel across the country. I thought it was the most
wonderful thing in the world that people would actually
listen to me sing, and when we got matching outfits, I
was sure I'd died and gone to heaven.

The summer of my junior year in high school, the
Continentals went to Europe. Daddy didn't want me to
go with them. We all had to pay our own way, and he
thought it was the dumbest thing he'd ever heard of for

people to *pay* to go work all summer. But, after much pleading from me and from Mother, he finally relented and allowed me to go.

I think Daddy was also afraid that if I went off to Europe I would no longer be his little girl and the closeness between us would suffer. He didn't want to let me out of the nest too soon for fear I wouldn't come back.

His fears were not totally groundless. Although I never stopped adoring Daddy, touring Europe with the Continentals opened my eyes to the vast array of possibilities in life outside of Tigard. My world view expanded and I began to question, "Why do I have to remain in Tigard all my life?"

That same summer I read the first thirty pages of Maxwell Maltz's *Psycho-Cybernetics*. It was not a Christian book, but it opened for me a whole new way of thinking. It shattered the remaining barriers in my mind, and I realized that I was valuable as a human being and that I needed to have no limits other than those I imposed on myself.

I have no idea today what those first thirty pages said, but whatever it was, it was revolutionary to my mind at the time. I got braces on my teeth, lost twenty pounds, took voice lessons, and broke up with the boy I had been dating for four years. I realized that if we married, it would just be out of habit and not because we loved each other or because either of us ignited any fire in the other's spirit.

For the first time I realized that I had a spirit, too—that I was more than just a body and a mind. I was a living, glorious creature of God. In spite of all my religious training, I had somehow never realized that. No one had ever told me that I was special to God—that I was a unique creation with my own set of talents and abilities. My background had taught me that to be spiritual meant to be passive, to accept my station in life, and never try to change or improve it. It meant never dreaming dreams, never pushing across the boundaries of the human spirit, never grasping who you are in Christ and what your destiny is as a child of God. It took a non-Christian book to awaken that knowledge in me.

It was shortly after that that I first began to hear of Oral Roberts University. My brother had gone to Northwest College near Seattle, Washington, and had met a girl there named Joan Moxley. He dated her for a long time and began bringing her home on weekends. She and I became good friends, and our family became good friends with her family. The Moxleys lived in Sweethome, Oregon, just a couple of hours away from Tigard. We would go down there to visit them on weekends or they would come to visit us. Joan's father, Homer, liked my singing, and he invited me several times to sing at his church.

He would sit me down on Sunday afternoon and talk to me about my plans for the future. He'd say to me, "You have a talent and you need to do something with it." He was a member of the Board of Regents at ORU, and he began telling me about the university.

I didn't know much about Oral Roberts, but when Homer began sharing with me Oral's dream of building a university where Christians would be trained to be the best in their chosen fields and would become missionaries not just in Africa or South America but in the board rooms of New York, the offices of Chicago, and the classrooms of Phoenix, I was enthralled.

Oral was affirming those things that were beginning to dawn in my spirit. He brought everything that I had been discovering about myself and the way I wanted to live into focus. He was saying that I could love Jesus and still become all that I could be in His name and take my place in the world community.

I had never heard that before, but I knew instinctively that it was true, and I responded immediately. I knew from then on that no matter what it took to get there, I wanted to be a part of ORU.

Daddy fought furiously against the whole idea. He did not like Oral Roberts, he did not want me going to a college so far away, and he thought it was crazy to enroll in a school that hadn't even been built yet. But I was determined to go.

Mother tried valiantly to get Daddy to change his mind—but to no avail. When it became apparent that he would not support me financially, Homer arranged for a scholarship for me.

Daddy still remained adamant in his opposition, and right up to the time I left we had terrible fights in which he absolutely forbade me to go. My decision was made more difficult by the fact that his arthritis had flared up, leaving him crippled and in a wheelchair. The doctor's prognosis was grim, and I wrestled with tremendous guilt at leaving him when he was so sick. Nevertheless, I believed I was doing the best thing for both of us. It wasn't Daddy's love that caused his opposition; it was his insecurity. Neither of us knew what the future would hold. We just knew that it would totally change our relationship.

The day I left, Daddy went with me to the train station. I remember him sitting there in his wheelchair crying. I knelt down in front of him, took his crippled hands in mine, and looked into his eyes. "Daddy, I know you're not going to understand this," I told him, "but I've got to go and I'm sorry you feel this way. I love you." I kissed his cheek, which was moist with tears. He didn't say anything, so I got up, gathered my bags, and boarded the train.

As the train pulled away from the station, I took one final look at him out my window. He looked so frail and forlorn sitting there on the platform that my throat constricted and hot tears splashed down my face onto the collar of my new red blouse.

He knew and I knew that things would never be the same. He was going to die and if I was ever going to have a chance at life, I was going to have to make it. Try as he would, Daddy couldn't give it to me.

He lived two and one-half more years, and during that time he did come to ORU, saw what I was so involved in, and gave me his blessing. He told me, "I'm sorry I tried to hold you back. You made the right decision."

I didn't know that September afternoon if I would ever hear those words from Daddy, but a fire had been ignited in my spirit and I couldn't quench it. I knew as the train rushed down the tracks, its wheels clicking rhythmically along the grade, that just as surely I was rushing into the greatest adventure of my life.

CHAPTER THREE

──*The Young Zealots*──

Right outside my dorm room window there was an oil well that pumped every night, tic-tic-tic-ummp. It had a musical quality to it, and I often lay awake listening and thinking how wonderful it was to be at ORU.

Everyone was so excited about being there, and we all had such a sense of purpose. It wasn't anything like going to college. It was more like founding a country.

My roommate that year was Dona Wantland. Dona was a couple of years older than I and we were distantly related. My father's brother had married her foster sister. When I was a child I got Dona's hand-me-down clothes, but I hadn't seen her in many years and had no idea that she was coming to ORU. She had been working for several years in New York City and had achieved some success as a singer and dancer. She had appeared in the chorus of several Broadway shows, but she had given up her career because she sincerely felt that the Lord wanted her to come to ORU.

Dona was beautiful, talented, and very intelligent. She was the perfect person for me to room with because she was mature and very serious about school. I never knew that you weren't supposed to be too serious about college, that you were supposed to just coast your way through and have a lot of parties, because Dona didn't have that mentality. I'd never been particularly interested in studies, but she was, so for recreation we studied and for a big night out we went in town to the library. Later I learned that there were other things one could do in college that were considerably more fun than our big study-parties.

We were both music majors, both curious about the world, both extremely idealistic and both totally committed to Oral's dream. We sang in the choir and in special musical groups, and we had a lot of classes together. We gobbled up books and we would sit up until three and four in the morning talking about ideas.

Dona and I became close friends with two other girls who lived down the hall from us, Hope Sutherland and Beverly Hubbard.

Hope and I came from very similar backgrounds. She had been raised in the Pentecostal Holiness Church and, when I first met her, was very religious. She was trying to break out of the mold of her past, too, and she had a mischievous streak which she tried very hard to keep from surfacing because it went against her "religious" training. She was an only daughter with two brothers, as I was. We were both slightly overweight and thought of ourselves as totally unattractive. Hope was one of those sweet persons that the boys always flocked around because she would listen sympathetically to their problems and sort of mother them.

Beverly looked and sounded just like Julie Andrews with dark hair, and she could imitate her precisely. She would fly through the dorm singing, "Raindrops on roses and whiskers on kittens. . . ." She was very theatrical but bright and, like the rest of us, terribly idealistic.

Beverly was a scholarship student also and never had much money, but she always had enough to send to someone who had less. She was totally unimpressed by wealth and had very little interest in possessions of any kind. She never went on shopping sprees and although she was always dressed very neatly, she wore the same two or three dresses over and over. She had one navy blue jumper that she wore so often the rest of us got tired of seeing it. One day Dona and I took it out of her closet and gave it away. Beverly had one of the purest, most giving hearts of anyone I have ever known, and she had a very deep, very sweet walk with the Lord.

The four of us spent all our time together, forming a sort of ORU "Gang of Four." We were all terribly intense and idealistic and saw ourselves as the true defenders of the faith.

At the end of my freshman year we expanded the group to include Joyce Tyson, the daughter of ORU's chaplain, Tommy Tyson. Joyce was different from the rest of us. A wonderfully flamboyant person, she made Auntie Mame look tame. She had excellent taste in clothes and she always had matching shoes and purses and a lot of Angora sweaters. She wore red lipstick before it was stylish, and red nail color. She was very open, very straightforward and could be rather intimidating at times. She was the most outrageous member of our group, and also the funniest, but she didn't feel the same sense of destiny as the rest of us. Quite simply, she had come to ORU to be educated. Consequently, she didn't have the same desire to change things. We were all so intense and so serious that Joyce provided a needed comic balance.

The five of us didn't date much. We did have a lot of male friends, most of whom were music students, and we all did things as a group. We were never trouble-makers, in the traditional sense of the word, but we played our share of practical jokes and pranks like normal college students.

One time Beverly and I got mad at something the two boys we were interested in had done, so we decided to retaliate. In Oklahoma, in the spring, when the outside lights came on at night, June bugs gravitated by the hundreds around the bulbs. We gathered about a hundred and fifty of them, put them in a box, wrapped it up, and carried it over to the music room where we knew Larry and Stan were practicing.

We walked in, handed them the present, and said, "We just want you guys to know how much we appreciate you, so we brought you this little gift. It's kind of personal, though, so would you please wait until we leave to open it?"

They were so sure of themselves that like idiots they believed us. When they opened that box, June bugs flew all over the room, all over them, and into the piano. We didn't hear the end of that for days.

But our pranks were few and far between. Most of my first two years of ORU were marked by work.

The university was still in its infant stage, and there was a constant need for money to complete the construction. Oral knew that we were his best advertisement. The appearance of a group of ORU students singing the praises of the university was a sure-fire money raiser.

By the mid-sixties, campus rebellion was escalating swiftly, and many parents were frightened and confused at the televised images of student protest that filled their living rooms each night. By contrast, we radiated a wholesome idealism and decency. We embodied the values of many middle-class Christians, and they were eager to support a university which promoted order and morality at a time when so many schools seemed to be surrendering to anarchy and indecency.

And we were glad to promote ORU, because we truly believed in the dream. Like most converts, we were zealous in our attempts to bring others into the fold.

We carried incredible schedules—attending classes during the day, putting in several hours of practice each afternoon, singing at Partners' meetings and seminars at night, getting back to the dorm just before curfew and then studying till early morning. Many times guests at the Partners Weekends stayed in our dorms. We *all* worked, *all* the time.

Effie Creel, our dorm mother, lived across the hall from Dona and me. Some mornings when our throats were raw from singing and we were so exhausted we thought we couldn't get out of bed, she would bring us hot tea with honey and lemon in it. She clucked over us like a mother hen over her baby chicks, but we loved her for it.

Invariably, after about a month of this pace, we would collapse from exhaustion and have to take a few days off from classes and meetings to recuperate. Then we would begin the whole cycle over again. It was an excruciating but exhilarating way to live.

By the middle of the fall semester of my second year at ORU, the pace had begun to get to me. I was simply tired of working so hard. The success of our efforts surrounded us. The university had grown from three small buildings to seven, and student enrollment had tripled. It was gratifying to see such visible, concrete results, but I was burned out.

Also, I was beginning to be disturbed by some of the things I saw happening around me. The dream of ORU had captured me so completely that I had poured my life into it for more than a year. It was the first thing that I had ever found that was worth living and dying for, and to me it was indescribably precious. I thought the dream was pure and holy, and I became very upset when it appeared to me that it was being packaged and sold like a box of breakfast cereal. I had no real concept of how much money it took to build and operate a university, but I believed that if God had called it into being, He could pay the bills without resorting to manipulative marketing methods. It produced rebellion in me as well as tremendous grief and anger. I was so angry that the very people who had been given the privilege of having the dream would turn around and, to my way of thinking, abuse it.

In retrospect I think I may have been a little like Don Quixote tilting at his imaginary windmills, but at the time I felt more like Joan of Arc. Dona, Hope, Beverly, and I would meet in my room and cry and gripe and sometimes pray for hours.

Dona was very articulate and outspoken. She never hesitated to say exactly what she thought about any faculty or administration member, or Oral himself, if he stepped out of line. We had fried Oral often, but he was not our only target. We genuinely loved Oral, even though his actions infuriated us at times. There were other members of the administration, however, whom we just couldn't tolerate. We didn't even consider them safe to have around ORU because we thought they had sold out to Madison Avenue. We'd say to each other, "How can Oral hire them? Doesn't he know?" Our biggest fear in those days was not sinning; it was selling out.

Many years later, after I had married and most of our little group had moved back to Tulsa, we got together for lunch at the Southern Hills Country Club where Oral was a member, and where Richard and I belonged. We talked about our ideals until we suddenly realized where we were. Then we laughed and said, "How did we get here? If this isn't selling out, I don't know what is. Tell me that money and power can't buy you."

But, as students, we were completely protective of the University. We didn't want anything to mar its image. One night a group of us returned home from a symphony concert and discovered a six-pack of beer which had been left on the trunk of a car and empty beer cans scattered around the parking lot. We were horrified. "What if the press should see this?" we thought. "They would say all kinds of horrible things about this wonderful place." So we gathered up all the cans, put them in paper bags, and carted them away. We were such zealots that we didn't want anything to blacken the name of the university.

I sometimes think we carried things a little too far, but we felt we had an investment in ORU. We were working and helping to build it. We were singing and raising money right along with Oral. He'd preach and we'd sing. We had no conception of normal college life. For us it was just "the dream." We had laid down our lives for it and said, "Here, build on me." And because we had given so much to it, when the emphasis began to shift and the dream was not held so dear, we became irritated.

There was always so much hype about the university and we resented it. We felt the dream was pure and obviously of God and did not need the kinds of marketing techniques that were beginning to seep in.

If we had confined our protests to prayer, we might have seen more lasting results, and we certainly would have avoided a great deal of trouble. But when God didn't seem to be getting the message, we decided to take things into our own hands.

We began voicing our dissent publicly, writing letters to the editor of the school paper protesting some of the public relations activities that we thought were manipulative and deceitful. We soon developed a reputation as troublemakers, which was ironic in view of our zeal to protect the university. But it was our zeal, uncoupled as it was with grace, which got us into trouble.

The climax came in the fall semester of my sophomore year.

Several of us music students had joined Oral's Crusade Teams on a tour of Brazil during the summer. The services had been exciting, with many people saved and healed. I had never seen such an awesome display of God's power. All of us had been awed by what God had done, and we were thrilled to be a part of it.

But when we returned to ORU, the *Abundant Life* magazine ran several stories about the Crusade which greatly exaggerated what had happened. We thought the magazine writers had inflated the number of people who had been saved and had recounted miracles that we weren't sure had occurred.

We were outraged, particularly because we thought the whole affair was so stupid and unnecessary. The Crusade had truly been wonderful. There were enough people saved and enough miracles to be impressive without having to invent new ones.

Among ourselves we began calling the magazine the *Abundant Lie*, and we wrote letters to the editor protesting the articles. Rumors started traveling around campus that we were threatening to burn the magazine in the parking lot and call the *Tulsa Tribune* to witness the event.

When Oral heard about our threatened bonfire, he was furious. He called us into his office and gave us a verbal lashing. In the first place, he said, we had no right to go to the newspapers without first having made our complaints known to him. We had convicted him without a trial and he did not appreciate it. He called our behavior irresponsible and immature and not in keeping with the standards ORU expected from its students.

Our cocky defiance crumpled under his withering attack. He said he should expel all of us. But he understood that our actions, as wrong as they were, were motivated by a sincere desire to seek the truth and to hold the university accountable to the values it was emphasizing. He told us the articles would be corrected and that he hoped a conversation of this sort would never again be necessary.

Then he dismissed us and we left, genuinely chagrined and considerably less defiant. We knew that we had come within a hair's breadth of being dismissed from school.

Oral was as good as his word, and the next stories published in *Abundant Life* were in keeping with what we remembered as having happened. The whole affair left us subdued and effectively put an end to our rebellion.

Dona, Hope, and Beverly left ORU the next year. Hope transferred to the University of Tulsa, as did Dona. After working in Tulsa for a year, Beverly went to Poland to study. But they have all returned to Tulsa and are, in some ways, still bound to ORU. At age thirty-five we are all still desperately in love with Oral's dream. We still believe in it, although we feel at times we're almost the last people in the world who do. It was a love/hate relationship from day one and it has remained so.

Had it not been for the tragic events that occurred in

my life, I would still be there too, fighting for the dream, searching through the maze of buildings to find the vision. The greatest disappointment in my life came a few years later when I realized that the dream had died or had changed and I was part of another world, already an anachronism and obsolete.

I never graduated from ORU, and I have often thought if Oral could have known what was to happen in our lives, he would have expelled me that fall when I was a student. It certainly would have saved all of us a lot of pain.

As it was, when I finally left ORU eleven years later, it was with a decree instead of a degree.

CHAPTER FOUR

Wedding Plans

"Have you heard the latest?" Hope asked, lounging in my doorway.

"No, what's happening now?" I said without looking up from my books. I was sitting at my desk trying to do a little last-minute cramming for a psychology exam.

"Richard Roberts is coming to ORU."

"You mean Oral's son?" She had my attention now. She sauntered into the room and plopped down on my bed.

"The very same."

"What's he doing here?" I asked. "I thought he was at Kansas University."

"Rumor has it that he didn't do so well at KU so he's come home to give it one last shot here."

"Well, I hope they don't make a big deal out of it. He probably thinks he's a big man on campus already," I said scornfully.

"I don't think they're going to," Hope said. "I'm really surprised he's even here. I've heard he's a real playboy and likes to keep a safe distance between himself and God."

"Great," I muttered, as I returned to my books. "That's just what we need around here."

Hope's predictions turned out to be accurate. Richard's enrollment was treated with very little fanfare by the university, and most of us viewed him with studied indifference.

I thought he was sort of cute but spoiled and a real lightweight when it came to being serious about anything important. We all knew that he wanted to be a Broadway musical star, and we thought, "Good, that's the place for him. We are serious believers here—out to change the world. So let him go play fluff if he wants to, but leave us alone." Dona went out with him once, and she thought he was a cute boy but nobody to be taken too seriously.

There was more than a little arrogance in our attitude toward Richard. We still saw ourselves as the defenders of ORU's spirituality, and it was beneath our dignity to react to the last name of Roberts. We did have a lot of respect for his mother and father, but we just didn't think we had a lot in common with Richard.

At that time, the music department had formed a singing group called the Collegians, which was the forerunner of the World Action Singers. Richard and I had both auditioned and been accepted. One night after rehearsal he asked if I'd like to go get something to eat with him, and I found myself saying I would . . . to the surprise of most of my friends.

The truth was, I was secretly flattered that he had asked me. He had such a reputation as a playboy that I knew he wasn't asking me out because he was impressed with the depth of my spirit, and he was, after all, very handsome.

We went to Pennington's Drive-In and sat and talked in his beige Chevy Malibu. It was early December and the weather was cold. Over hamburgers, Dr. Peppers, and black-bottom pie we discussed our life's goals.

"I've always wanted to be a night club singer," he told me. "I sang at the Starlight Theatre in Kansas City when I was at KU, and I enjoyed it. But I really just want to do what God wants me to do."

For some reason, I believed him. He was such a gentleman, so polite and so sweet, that he took me by surprise. In my own tactful way I told him I was surprised, that I hadn't expected his value system to accommodate God's will or for that to even be a consideration in his life. When he asked if we could pray together before he took me back to the dorm, I thought, "Maybe there is hope for him."

Richard and I dated the rest of that year. He was fascinated by me because I was independent and arrogant, and because I thought differently from most of the girls he had dated. At first, he thought I came from a wealthy family. He couldn't believe that a scholarship student would say the things about the administration that I did. My idealistic rebelliousness intrigued him.

I was disarmed by Richard's charm. He had a temper and could be petulant and demanding, but he was also sweet and fun to be with. He was handsome, he talked nicely, he had been in private schools most of his life, and he knew how to treat people politely. His social graces were impeccable, and he always showed me great kindness and respect.

Our relationship was basically uneventful. We went to movies, listened to concerts, and sang together. Richard is a very methodical person. If he decides to date you, he spends whatever free time he has with you. If he's not doing something else, he's with you. Richard is not a loner. He hates even to eat by himself, and he likes to have company in most of his activities. He has never been one for going out with the boys very much, so whomever he was dating had to fill his needs for companionship.

I thought there was a great sense of destiny about our

meeting and liking each other so well. It didn't really surprise me that Richard Roberts would like me because I had always known that God was going to use me. What better place than ORU?

We were both operating off pretty shaky self-images then, he in particular, because he didn't really know who he was or whether or not he could step into Oral's world, and he was not sure if he could carve out a world for himself.

Richard had so much potential at that time, I felt, and the rebellion he had experienced had been good for him because it had caused him to examine who he was. He was honestly searching in those days.

We'd take long walks and talk; or, rather, he'd talk and I'd listen and try to understand what was happening inside of him.

"I don't know what I'm going to do, Patti," he'd say. "I've got another year here and then I graduate and I don't know what I'm going to do with my life. I'd like to sing on Broadway but only if it's God's will for me." I know the phrase "God's will" has been used so often and so broadly that it has become a catch-all, but at that time we were sincerely trying to be in tune with God's desires.

He let out a long sigh. "I know Dad would like me to join him in the ministry but I'm just not ready to do that yet. All my life I've been Oral Roberts' son, but what about me? What about Richard? Why can't I have a life apart from my dad?"

In my naïveté, I think I did Richard great harm during this very crucial time in his life. I encouraged him to become involved with Oral's ministry because at the time that seemed to me to be the most spiritual thing to do. I had grown up with the mentality that there wasn't anything better or closer to the heart of God than being religiously famous. I didn't know how costly fame could be.

At that point I didn't know Oral very well either. I didn't know how important the empire was to him or how protective he was tempted to become when he felt it was threatened. I didn't recognize that he could be measuring his value *to* God by what he could do *for* God, and I didn't see the hurt that his absorption with the ministry was causing his family.

But Richard was keenly aware of the emotional land mines. He had suffered a great deal as Oral's son. He had been both the recipient and the victim of his father's success. He knew the price it had extracted from their family.

For most of his life, Richard had been distanced—both physically and emotionally—from his father. Oral really loved his children, but, as is often the case with famous fathers, the demands of his career had a hurtful effect on his children's development. Richard had been hurt too much. He had been poured into too many molds in his life, and, when I met him, he was struggling to find the courage to break free.

I think he resisted joining Oral in the ministry because he recognized, whether consciously or not, that to do so would mean relinquishing his last chance to establish an identity for himself. He knew intuitively that to join his father could spell the death of his self, and that terrified him. His fears were later to prove well-founded but I didn't know any of that then. I believe that in my innocence I may have preempted the distinctive work of the Holy Spirit in Richard's life that could have led to the unfolding of his own unique calling.

It all seemed so simple and wonderful to me. In my

mind, Richard was close to the university, close to Oral, and thereby close to Jesus. I thought if he was close to Jesus, he'd be close to me and I could love him and be there, and he could love me and we'd do wonderful things for God.

I was very sincere, but I didn't understand that God had placed unique gifts in Richard and Patti and that He might have a higher destiny for us. I couldn't imagine any higher destiny than working for ORU. I was still in love with Oral's dream. I didn't realize that God could give us our own dream.

That summer I went to Europe on a singing tour. Richard decided at the last minute to stay home and work at ORU's radio station. Midway through the tour, Oral and Evelyn flew over to join us. Richard, knowing that I loved Dr. Pepper, asked Evelyn to bring me a can on which he had written, "As often as you drink of this, think of me." I thought that was an amusing gesture on his part, and I was charmed by it. Evelyn and I had several opportunities to talk during that time, and I began to develop a genuine love for her.

Richard and I corresponded throughout the summer, and one day while we were in England, I received a telegram from him that read: "I have decided that we will get married this Christmas. Love, Richard." He called me that night and I agreed to marry him.

My friends were horrified. They all liked Richard and thought it was wonderful that he was turning around and becoming interested in God, but they didn't think he was the person for me. They told me, "This man does not love you and you do not love him. This is not right for you, Patti." But their advice fell on deaf ears. I had convinced myself that it must be God's will for me to marry

Richard. After all, I reasoned, I wanted to serve God, and what better way than by marrying a Roberts?

After I came home, Richard and I went to the Louisiane, one of Tulsa's better restaurants, to celebrate our official engagement. Over a candlelight dinner, we sipped cokes like two teenagers and talked about our future. Richard gave me an engagement ring—a beautiful one-carat diamond in a simple gold setting.

After dinner we went by to see Evelyn and Oral. They congratulated us and were very sweet. I think they were relieved that Richard was marrying a Christian girl and had given up the idea of being a nightclub singer.

Everything about our engagement looked right. If there was ever any chance that Richard might join his father in ministry, he had to have a suitable wife, and I looked perfect for the part. I was just feisty enough to keep things from getting boring, just spiritual enough to be successful in the role, and seemed just enough like Evelyn that Richard could be like Oral. I don't think any of this was an overt thought on Richard's part. He was running purely on intuition then.

The only problem was that neither Richard nor I were mature enough to get married. We didn't know much about love, and we knew little about commitment. We were two kids in love with the idea of being in love and sincerely trying to be in love with each other.

It's very easy to say "I love you," and people often say it when they want to love somebody. "I love you" was a statement of faith for us. We said it because we couldn't figure out any reason not to say it.

I happened into Richard's life at the right time with the right qualifications. I think he loved what I was, not me. And I loved who he was. Here was a man who was going to give up a Broadway career for Jesus—a man who said, "I don't care about the wealth or power of my father. I care about Jesus." Those were intoxicating phrases to me. I just didn't realize how long he had been a Roberts and what that had cost him and how that had colored his perception of life and love.

As the wedding grew closer, I began to have serious second thoughts about what we were doing and I vacillated back and forth. One day I wanted to marry Richard and the next day I didn't. The confusion I experienced really had nothing to do with anything Richard did or didn't do. I couldn't put my finger on exactly what was wrong. I just sensed that something about our relationship wasn't right and I was terrified of doing the wrong thing. I also had a real sense of guilt because I couldn't make my heart match my intellectual decision and I couldn't understand why. Richard sensed my ambivalence and it frustrated him.

One night about two months before the wedding, I became so depressed that I poured out my anguish in a poem. As soon as I finished I raced over to the music department, hoping to catch one of my friends still practicing. I found Larry in one of the practice rooms. Bursting in on him, I rushed up to the piano and said, "Larry, start playing in the key of G. I've got something I want you to hear." We had often created impromptu songs together so he was not particularly surprised by my request. As he began to play, I sang:

> The night has been too long,
> Too dark for searching eyes to see.
> The winds have come and blown
> The candle of my dreams from me.
> Where is my new song to sing?
> What good can this new day bring?

Where are all those beautiful things
Life promised it would give?
· ·
The salty rain that drenches me,
Drowning joys I hoped would be,
Falls from my eyes and I can see
The wasted years that follow me.
I can't accept this useless fate,
One void of purpose and dreams grown great.
There's one last chance, just one for me.
Jesus, can You make me what I long to be?*

It was a cry of desperation from the depths of my being. When I finished, I said nothing to Larry but walked out of the room and slammed the door.

It wasn't until just before my divorce that I was able to finish that poem. For the next ten years I would say those words to Jesus several times a year. "Can you make me what I long to be? I'm trying so hard to fit into your plans. I want so badly to do Your will. Can You do it for me?" It took many years and a lot of pain before I even began to have any clear understanding of how and why God uses people. His main interest is in our relationship with Him, our knowing Him, not our employment. Our true call is to know Him. When serving Him preempts knowing Him, we've got a problem.

It was an excruciatingly lonely period for me. I had no one that I could really talk to. All of my friends thought I was crazy. They thought that both Richard and I had gotten caught up in the momentum of the relationship, and they were upset that they couldn't pull us out of it. Daddy, who had always given me sound advice about my boyfriends, had died the year before and Mama had been seriously injured in a car accident just two weeks after Richard and I became engaged.

I tried to talk to Richard, and he was always very comforting. He'd hold me in his arms and say, "I know you love me and it's going to be all right. You'll see." But he was whistling in the dark, too.

Things reached a breaking point one afternoon several weeks before the wedding. Richard and I were going shopping, and he had come by the dorm to pick me up. It always irritated Richard that I never wore blue jeans. He thought I was trying to be super spiritual, but I just didn't own any jeans and I was embarrassed to tell him that. So, this afternoon, as usual, I wore a dress.

When I came down the stairs, he was standing in the lobby in blue jeans, and I could tell he was angry about something. He didn't say much as we walked across to the parking lot. When we reached the car, he just stood by it and glared at me. When I asked him what was wrong, he grabbed my shoulders and began shaking me and yelling, "What's the matter with you anyway? You think you're too good to wear blue jeans? Why can't you ever relax and act like a normal person?"

I was stunned. I had never seen Richard act like that before, and it frightened me. I began to cry.

The sight of my tears seemed to snap him out of it. "Oh, Patti, don't cry. I'm sorry. I didn't mean that. I don't know what came over me," he said.

"That's okay," I sniffed. "I'll go upstairs and change. I don't have any blue jeans, but I'll put on some slacks."

"No, you don't have to change," he said, but I was already out of the car.

We went on to the mall and neither of us mentioned the incident the rest of the afternoon, but shortly after that I decided I wasn't going to marry him. I was beginning to have serious doubts about his Christian commitment. His outbursts of temper, his reluctance to join his father in the ministry, the fact that he still cussed occasionally and liked to have a few beers every now and then with his friends all led me to question whether he had really given his life to Christ or whether he was still playing games with God. I decided to break off the engagement so that I could try to sort out my feelings and seek the Lord's will once more.

(I realize now that my judgment of Richard and his commitment to God was very shallow and legalistic. I judged a person's spirituality largely on the basis of his or her external conduct. It didn't occur to me that a person could do all of the right things and still have a heart far removed from God. Or that he or she could have a very deep and genuine relationship with Jesus and not conform to a rigid set of rules.)

I gave him back the ring and told him the engagement was off. The effect on Richard was immediate and dramatic. He has told it many times and both Oral and Evelyn have recounted it in their autobiographies.

Richard went home as soon as I broke the news to him. Oral was in California, and Evelyn was home by herself. He walked in and without any small talk blurted out, "Mother, I am in trouble."

Evelyn said, "What's wrong, Richard?"

He replied, "Something's happened to Patti. She can't get it through her head that I love her. She's going to call off the wedding."

He kept on talking, pouring out his hurt and confusion. When he finished, he asked his mother to pray for him, and while they were praying something broke loose inside of him. When they finished, he said, "Everything's all right now. I don't want to give up Patti, but if that's the way it must be, then okay. Regardless, I'm going to live my life completely for God." Then he called and told Oral of his decision.

Up to this point, even while he was professing to want to serve God, Richard had still shied away from committing himself fully to joining Oral's ministry. But now, he told Oral, "Instead of feeling like you're always on my back, I think of myself as by your side." He had truly come home in every sense of the word.

Now I think Richard and I both assumed that to be in God's work meant to be in Oral's work. I don't think he has a point of reference outside of the Oral Roberts Association. So when he was out of the camp, he was a sinner; when he was inside the camp, he was going to serve God by serving Oral. Given his background, that's a very logical assumption and one which I encouraged at the time, but it has cost him a great deal not to realize that it doesn't have to be that way.

Later, Richard expanded on what had happened that afternoon in Evelyn's kitchen. "When I discovered that I hadn't really committed my life to the Lord the way I really should, I saw myself in a different light. It took almost losing what I wanted most to make me turn around and say, 'God, I will do what You want me to whether I keep Patti or not.'"

I was always a little embarrassed when Richard gave this testimony because it made me sound like such a little saint, which I was not. After we were married, we'd visit Richard's grandmother and she'd always say to me, "Honey, who are you?" I'd say, "Granny, I'm Patti," and then she'd exclaim, "Praise God, you're the one who turned Richard around." Her mind was a little foggy but her religious fervor was still hot. However, I never felt I truly deserved credit for Richard's decision.

While Richard was praying with Evelyn, I was praying too, and I honestly did feel a release. I still did not feel joyous about the wedding, but something happened. To this day, I don't know whether God really did speak to me that afternoon or whether my perceptions at that point were just so distorted that I couldn't hear the voice of God clearly.

But, I did feel peace about the situation and I couldn't wait to find Richard and tell him about my decision. I met him the next day before class, but before I had a chance to tell him my news, he grabbed my arm and began talking excitedly about what had happened to him.

I just stared at him. I couldn't believe what I was hearing. "Oh, Richard, that's wonderful," I cried, flinging my arms about his neck. "God's timing is so perfect. While you were praying with your mother, I was praying too, and I believe everything is going to be okay."

Richard pulled me close to him and kissed me tenderly. As I buried my head in his chest, I said a silent thank you to God. Surely this was the answer to the uneasiness in my heart, I thought. God knew that Richard hadn't made a total commitment of his life, and that was why I had no peace about our getting married. Now that Richard had taken that step, I felt sure that our love for each other could blossom and we could have a wonderful life together.

When I think back on that scene today, I never know whether to laugh or to cry. Richard and I were such innocents. We were totally ignorant of the sacrifices and commitment that are required to build a good marriage. We just assumed that if we loved each other and we both loved the Lord that He would protect us and everything would work out all right. And no one told us any differently.

If we had had adequate premarital counseling, we might have avoided a lot of heartache. Any competent counselor would have spotted our immaturity and our unrealistic ideas about marriage. He might also have seen the great chasms that existed between our personalities, our perceptions of life, the way we dealt with conflicts and our expectations of marriage. We were opposites in so many ways, and while it is true that opposites attract, it requires a great deal of understanding, patience, and plain hard work for them to build an enduring relationship.

In one sense, we entered into our marriage blind. A good premarital counselor could have opened our eyes to some of the pitfalls we faced and might have encouraged us to wait until we both had a little more maturity. At least, we would have had a more sober, realistic view of what we were doing. But the counseling sessions we had were very brief and superficial. No one at ORU was going to tell Richard Roberts that he couldn't marry anyone he wanted to, and we never considered going outside the university to seek counsel. In fairness, I must also add that Richard and I both could present a very self-assured, very glib exterior. We knew all of the biblical phrases about marriage, and we could present a very convincing case that we knew what we were doing. Unfortunately, no one ever questioned us.

So, on that October day, convinced that God had placed His blessing on our plans, we joined hands and walked across campus, excitedly making plans. Our wedding was less than a month away.

CHAPTER FIVE

Marriage under Threat

We were married on November 27, 1968, having decided on a Thanksgiving wedding rather than a Christmas wedding. It was a cold, gray, foreboding afternoon—the kind of day to make you wonder what you had done so wrong that you should have this on your wedding day.

The miserable weather outside matched the mood of the wedding party inside. It was one of the strangest occasions I've ever attended. Everyone was nervous, as I suppose they are at most weddings, but there was no joy in the atmosphere.

My brothers were laughing because they thought it was ludicrous. I was crying because I was terrified. Richard looked like he was in the ozone layer, just floating around. Evelyn and my mother seemed hopeful and Oral looked as if he had lost his last friend in the world.

My family was all rather intimidated by the Robertses. There we were, the four of us, just sort of ordinary people being integrated into this powerful family and wondering what on earth was going to happen to us.

My brothers covered their apprehension by cracking jokes. Alan said we should have had the wedding in the big tent and wondered if we could have a little healing service after the ceremony. Ronnie asked why I carried a bouquet instead of palm branches.

They thought Richard was a little starchy but they liked him. Ronnie and Richard got along especially well and became warm, deep friends. Later Ron worked for Richard as his executive assistant for years and subsequently served as director for the family practice clinic at ORU.

To make matters worse, the bridesmaids' dresses I had ordered had not arrived, and as the ceremony grew closer, it looked as if I might have to walk down the aisle by myself. I was too numb to care at that point, but my bridesmaids were verging on panic. My mother was calling the store, frantically trying to locate them, with little success. Finally, an hour before the wedding, the dresses arrived by UPS. Fortunately they needed no alterations beyond what could be done with a safety pin or a needle and thread. They were a deep, deep red velvet—the color of American beauty roses, trimmed in heavy white lace at the throat, the bodice, and around the wrists.

We had a very small wedding. Only twenty-three people, almost all of them family, attended. My sister-in-law, Joan, was the maid of honor, and Richard's youngest sister, Roberta, was the other bridesmaid. Richard's niece, Brenda Nash, was the flower girl. My older brother, Alan, gave me away. Richard's oldest brother, Ron, was the best man and my younger brother, Ron, was his other attendant.

My dress had an empire waist with a tight bodice and a pretty little high neck with lots of seed pearls on it. Seed pearl flowers covered the skirt and ran down the long train. I paid $120 for it and thought that was a tremendous amount of money for a dress you'd only wear once.

Little did I know I'd have that dress forever. As I have moved from house to house from city to city, I've always carefully kept it. I don't know what you do with a dress from a marriage that didn't work. It seems almost a sacrilege to throw it away, but the marriage turned out to be disposable. The dress is all packed away in huge gold boxes, free from dust and guaranteed not to yellow. When I look at it, it hurts that all that care is taken to preserve a dress when so little care was taken to preserve a family, but I guess it's easier to store a dress than to make a marriage work.

Of course, thoughts like those were the farthest thing from my mind as Mother helped me into the dress that afternoon.

When the ceremony finally started and it was time for me to walk down the aisle with Alan, he took my arm and said, "Are you sure you want to go through with this?"

I hesitated for just a second, then said, "Yeah, let's do it."

So we started out and all the way from the back door to the altar I prayed silently. "Lord, if this isn't Your will, could you just be kind to all of us and let me drop dead before I reach the altar?"

It was a sincere prayer. I didn't want to make a mistake, and at that point everything was so jangled and confused I honestly didn't know if I was doing the right thing or not. I didn't want to embarrass God by having a bad marriage.

I have since learned that if you don't know what to do, it's best not to do anything. Just wait. You don't have to wander around confused. James says in the first chapter of his epistle: "If any of you lack wisdom, let him ask God . . . and it shall be given him" (v. 5). God is faithful and He will direct us in no uncertain terms.

It would have been wonderful if either Richard or I had known that then. Richard had his doubts, too, but, having committed himself, he was determined to see it through. And there was a lot of pride on the line for both of us.

I kept telling myself, "If it's not right, we'll make it work. What could be so hard? I'm reasonable, he's reasonable, we like each other—" And when I got to the end of the aisle, I was still breathing, so we stood there and said, "I do."

Bob DeWeese, Oral's assistant evangelist, performed the ceremony and I could see the pages shake as he read the Scripture. My mother didn't cry that I know of, but Oral sobbed. Throughout the ceremony, we could hear these big s-n-i-f-f's behind us. It was one of the most mournful occasions I ever attended. Even our wedding pictures look grim. Everyone is standing around looking glum, with polite little smiles frozen on their faces.

The reception was held at Oral and Evelyn's house. Evelyn had arranged for a lovely dinner to be catered and had put out her nicest china and linens, with flowers on the tables.

The table in their dining room was almost banquet size and over the years at Christmas, Thanksgiving, and other holidays, we had many family dinners around it. All the sons- and daughters-in-law and grandchildren could fit around it, and we had a lot of happy times eating, talking, laughing and teasing each other, just enjoying being together. After dinner, Oral would take a package of Juicy Fruit gum, put all five sticks in his mouth at once, chew them until all the sugar was gone. Then he would put them on his plate and he was finished. That was dessert for him. When the sugar was gone from the Juicy Fruit, the dinner was over and we'd break up.

But tonight the dessert was the wedding cake. Richard and I cut it and posed for more pictures. Finally, we slipped away to change clothes and prepare to leave on our honeymoon.

Right before we left, Oral called us into his study. He closed the door, sat down in one of the armchairs facing the stone fireplace and began to cry.

Richard and I just stared at him, disconcerted. For several minutes no one said anything. The only sounds in the room were the logs crackling and hissing on the fire and the ticking of the clock on the mantel. Richard stared down at the floor and traced a pattern with his shoe in the burnt-orange carpet.

Finally Oral spoke. Addressing Richard, he announced that he had had a dream about him and me the night before. If either of us ever were to leave Oral's ministry or turn our backs on God, we'd be killed in a plane crash. That was his total message except to say he loved us both and that we should have a wonderful honeymoon. And of course . . . goodbye.

Richard and I were horrified. We couldn't imagine what we had done that had angered God so much that He would start our marriage off with a threat. It never occurred to us that maybe it wasn't God who had spoken, but Oral trying to manipulate us to protect the ministry.

The machine was already making unrealistic demands. Our marriage represented a new fork in the road for Oral. I think now that he was trying to make sure that our destination was the same as his, but we were too innocent to believe that he could have anything but pure motives. And, at that point in our lives, it was difficult for us to distinguish the voice of God from the voice of Oral—they sounded so much alike. So for many years, I accepted it as a fact that if I ever left the Roberts' ministry, God would kill me.

We had a 9:00 P.M. flight to San Antonio to catch and

Alan drove us to the airport. It was a silent ride most of the way. Alan had no idea what Oral had said to us, but he sensed that something was wrong. He tried to make cheerful conversation, and I made a feeble attempt to respond, but Richard just gripped my hand and stared morosely out the window into the darkness.

Once we boarded our flight, I had to make a real effort to sit calmly in my seat. As the plane climbed through the night sky and broke through the clouds to where the moon was, I wondered if we would ever land or if the plane would crash.

We finally arrived in San Antonio and caught a cab to our hotel—a lovely Spanish inn right on the Guadalupe. You could walk out the back door and down to the river, explore the colorful little shops in the Mexican bazaar, and eat authentic Mexican foods.

It was 2:00 A.M. when we finally got into our room. Bob Stamps, the ORU chaplain, had sent us a telegram saying he wished us well and God bless us both. I thought it was very sweet and saved it for years.

Our wedding night was both strange and funny. I think if all wedding nights were like it, no one would get married.

We were both very tired and began immediately to get ready for bed. Evelyn had given me a beautiful peignoir set as a wedding present and I decided to wear that. It was pure white, trimmed with pink satin and white lace.

Like most new brides, I had been looking forward eagerly to this night. For the first time in my life, I was going to make love to a man and it was going to be a wonderful thing to do. I hoped it would also help relieve some of the trauma of this day. Richard was going to love me, and maybe that would take this uneasiness out of my heart. Maybe by physically pouring out his love he could take the confusion and fear away from both of us. Maybe we could love it away.

My fantasies were interrupted abruptly when Richard looked up from the bed and said, "You know, you look fatter with your clothes off."

I was devastated. I was self-conscious about. my weight anyway. Now I wanted to hide—to cover my nakedness, both physical and emotional—from this man. I did not feel like an adored bride, a precious love object to my husband. I felt fat and unattractive, and I realized with a sinking feeling in the pit of my stomach that while we might make love on this night, we would not be lovers. We might be physically intimate, but there would be no real intimacy between us.

Richard seemed blissfully unaware of the effect his words had produced in me and urged me to come on to bed. I should have shared my feelings with him right then and cleared the air, but I was too hurt. So, I kept silent and we dutifully and rather timidly consummated our marriage.

We drifted off to sleep—or at least Richard did, but not before first depositing a quarter in the "Magic Fingers" machine attached to the bed. The Magic Fingers were supposed to act as a gentle massage, relaxing you and lulling you to sleep. They worked fine—in fact they worked too well. Three hours later they were still massaging the bed and I felt like the victim of the world's longest continuous earthquake. Richard never stirred. By 6:00 A.M. I had endured all the wonderfulness I could possibly stand. I scrambled under the bed, yanking at every wire I could find. I was determined to get that possessed bed stopped, one way or another. I finally found the right cord and got the machine halted. I climbed wearily back into bed, and by 6:15 A.M. I was lying peacefully—the bride asleep, at last.

When I awoke, the sun was streaming in through the sliding glass doors off the balcony and Richard was watching cartoons on television. We watched the Road Runner together, then went down and ate Thanksgiving dinner in the hotel dining room.

Two days later we were bored. So we cut short the honeymoon and came home. That should have been the first indication to us and to others that something was wrong with our marriage already. But we were such good performers that we convinced everybody that we knew what we were doing—and we almost convinced ourselves.

CHAPTER SIX

Two Frightened Children
in a Fantasy World

Richard and I set up housekeeping in one side of a duplex at 1005 East Forty-Second Street in Tulsa. It had two bedrooms, a little kitchen with an eating area, a living room and one bath.

We were both still attending school and he worked as a DJ at ORU's radio station. Richard had a trust fund, and we lived on a small advance from that plus what he made at the radio station. Our income that year was $9,000, and that seemed like an incredible amount of money to us. We had our Malibu, our television, a stereo, and a Maytag washer and dryer that Evelyn had given us for a wedding present.

Evelyn also let us put our living room furniture on her charge account. We picked out a hide-a-bed covered in a fine-striped gold and green and trimmed in pecan, two square pecan end tables that we used in lieu of a coffee table, and a hexagonal pecan lamp table. Evelyn also gave us an old chair of Oral's that we covered in greenish gold brocade.

In our bedroom we had a queen size bed and a pine chest which I covered in contact paper. I splurged and bought an eighty-five dollar bedspread with pink and red flowers on it. It seemed almost sinful to spend that much on a bedspread, but I later gave it to a girlfriend and she's still using it, so it must have been a good purchase.

In our extra bedroom we put our books, the television and the stereo, one chair, and an old red leatherette sofa that we had rescued from university storage.

Describing it now, it sounds as if we had wretched taste, but actually it all looked pretty good together. We had a lot of fun fixing up the house, improvising on our decor with a mixture of old, new, borrowed and rehabilitated furniture. It was a simple, sweet way to begin our lives together.

At the end of December we went to Haiti with Oral and the World Action Singers to do a crusade. While we were there we sang for Haiti's president, Papa Doc Duvalier. I remember walking up the steps of the presidential palace and seeing guards armed with machine guns surrounding the building. It was a chilling sight, and it made me realize how blessed we are to have the freedoms that we have in the United States.

Those first few months were lonely for both of us. Neither Richard nor I had many friends in Tulsa. My old college friends had all left town. Richard didn't have many friends because he had lived in Kansas and had only been in Tulsa a short time before we began dating. We eventually made new, married friends, but that took time.

Some nights I felt so alone I crawled up into Richard's lap, put my head on his shoulder, and cried. He tried to comfort me, but he was as lost and lonely as I was. Had either of us been less insecure, our loneliness could have brought us closer together. Instead it became the first crack in our union. It seemed like a tiny fissure at first, almost imperceptible, but over the following decade it would grow into a canyon so great that no one could bridge it.

Richard and I are both very emotional, very moody people, but he is more introverted while I am extroverted. I need constant reinforcement and interaction. I have to have emotional feedback. I like to air my feelings and in the process can sometimes become intimidating, although that is never my intent. Richard, on the other hand, tends to bottle things up inside him. He is uncomfortable, as many men are, with expressing his emotions. The more I insisted on confrontation, the more he retreated. But, instead of talking about our communication problems and exploring ways to work them out, we ignored them.

They didn't seem major at first. But the seeds of distrust, of hurt and resentment were being sown, and they would produce a bitter harvest. If we had just realized that major problems begin with minor irritations that are not dealt with constructively, we could have avoided a lot of unnecessary pain. That is so obvious that it seems incredible we could not have seen it. But it is the obvious things in life that we most often overlook.

In many ways Richard and I were like two frightened children, calling out to each other across the walls of the fortresses we had built around our hearts. Neither of us knew how to breach the walls, so we remained isolated, lonely, and afraid, even though both of us were desperate for love.

At that point, Richard and I were both committed to marriage, and with some reservations, we were committed to each other. There was a little flame of caring between us that, had it been nurtured, could have blazed into love.

What we needed most was time. Time to grow up. Time to establish our identities—both as individuals and as a couple. Time to see if we could lower our walls and learn to trust each other and to build a life together. But time was the one luxury we were never afforded.

I think now that if we had had a better sense of reality, we would have married, moved away someplace, finished our education, learned who we were, fallen deeply in love, and built a solid relationship between us. Then, had we felt it right to go back to work with Oral, we would have been strong enough and mature enough to realize what the issues were, what the odds were, what parts we could play and what parts we couldn't. But we never exercised that option.

In January, less than two months after we were married, Oral began his weekly television show, and Richard and I began our lives as professional newlyweds. After that, our chances for building a solid, satisfying relationship were greatly decreased. We were not ready either as individuals or as a couple for the pressures that celebrity status conferred on us. We were so naïve, we were caught up in the glamour and excitement of it but gave no thought to the cost it might extract.

Suddenly, we were forced to present a very unreal image to the world. Thousands of dollars and a carefully designed public image rested on our being happily married. We could not go on TV and say, "We are newlyweds and we believe that establishing a solid foundation for our life together takes precedence over the ministry, so we are going to leave the show for a few months or a year and establish our family. Pray for us."

Our mentality at that point would not have allowed us to do that. Neither of us was mature enough to see that we needed some time just for ourselves, and neither of us had a clear biblical understanding of the importance God places on family relationships. We sincerely, but wrongly, believed that ministry was the most important thing. So we built our marriage on the sand of wrong teaching. We created a public image and then worked very hard to make our private lives match it. But, unfortunately, the depth of our relationship never grew beyond what we presented to the public.

None of that was conscious on our part. We were too busy just trying to keep our heads above water. I had experienced three major changes in my life, one right after another. Getting married is in itself a major change that usually requires some period of adjustment. Marrying into a family as famous as the Robertses exacerbated the normal stresses, and beginning work on a national TV show six weeks after the wedding administered the final coup de grace. Everything happened so quickly I had no time to think or to prepare myself. I felt like a Cinderella who had suddenly been hit by the magic wand. One moment I was sitting on the pavement by the pumpkin, and the next I was riding away in the horse-drawn carriage with the prince at my side. It was exhilarating, but I felt disoriented much of the time.

The TV ministry brought with it much of the same excitement and idealism that had attended the founding of ORU. Once again we felt like pioneers, and we were. Oral had a vision to reach the unchurched with this TV show. But to do that he realized the program would have to be aired during prime time and it would have to have the look and musical sound of topflight productions. Working with producer Dick Ross and conductor Ralph Carmichael, he developed the format we would use in all of our prime time specials, which would be filmed at NBC studios in Burbank, California. They would have famous guests, special sets and wardrobes, and new, up-tempo music.

The first special was aired in March of 1969 with Mahalia Jackson as the special guest. It was a gamble. Religious programmers had never done anything quite like it. But it was an enormous success. In the years since then, many others have imitated it, but none have used it as effectively as Oral.

In contrast to the excitement of our professional lives, our personal lives were boring. Richard and I both worked so hard. We gave the best we had to the ministry, so we had very little left to give to each other. We didn't spend quality time together. We didn't nurture each other, or invest our lives in each other. We invested our lives in the TV show. It became our source—of money, of affirmation, of security and fulfillment. It also represented the only spiritual life we had together.

We were professional Christians. Our entire lives revolved around the ministry. We spent eight to ten hours a day working in a completely Christian environment. We sang and prayed together on TV. It was easy for us to be lulled into believing that we didn't need to spend time together in private devotions. It was a subtle trap and one that all those who work in full-time, paid ministry have to guard against. When Richard and I came home after a long day of taping, we did not read the Bible and pray together. If we had, we might have developed a clearer perspective on the ministry and what was happening to our marriage.

By 1971 we had moved into our first real house, 2929 East Seventy-eighth Place, a little Spanish house behind the university. It had three bedrooms, a kitchen, living room and den, complete with fireplace, and we felt terribly wealthy. By that time we were making $12,000 a year.

We also became parents that year. Richard and I had been trying to have a baby for about a year and a half but had had no success. I wanted a child desperately. I thought maybe if we had a baby it would bring Richard and me closer. When it became apparent that we were not going to be able to have a child ourselves, we decided to adopt one.

We first talked about adopting a child in December of 1970, and within two months, working through a private attorney, we had arranged to adopt Christine Michelle.

On February 21, 1971, we drove to a private airport south of Tulsa, where the lawyer had agreed to meet us. We parked the car and watched as a little brown and white plane circled and came in for a landing. It taxied up to us, and then the door opened and the attorney stepped out holding a tiny white bundle in his arms. He handed the bundle to me and said, "Here, Mama." I was afraid to even open it up. I just said, "Thank you," turned around, and walked away. I don't know what Richard said to him. I got in the car and waited for him. When he got in, we began to unwrap this incredible package of love that had been sent to us.

Under the blankets, all scrunched up, was this fat, bald-headed, blue-eyed baby. She was just gorgeous and we couldn't believe she was really ours.

We took her home and I sat down in the little blue nursery we had fixed up and began to rock her. Oral and Evelyn came over. Oral poked his head in the bedroom door and looked at me rocking her. He got great big tears in his eyes and couldn't say anything. He just went into the other room. Evelyn, of course, was an immediate grandma, wanting to hold her, feed her, change her. She wanted me to rest and not exert myself, exactly the same as if I'd just come home from the hospital.

Christi was such a joy to us, it was just unbelievable. She was a precious gift to us from God. We were so grateful to have her.

We took her on TV with us and were flooded with mail and baby gifts from all over the world. I outfitted about fourteen babies from it all. People were so lovely and the partners all expressed such love and concern over her. It was a wonderful time.

Two months after she arrived, Richard and I had to go to England for a previously scheduled meeting. We were gone about two weeks, and on the way back I became deathly ill. Everyone thought I had the flu but I couldn't seem to shake it. I began being sick every morning. Finally Evelyn said to me, "I think you're pregnant."

I just laughed at her and said, "Hey, it's me, the old girl who doesn't get pregnant, remember? I couldn't be, and besides, I have a baby. Why would anyone get pregnant when they have a baby?" About seven months later Julene Allison was born.

I had a very difficult pregnancy. In addition to horrible morning sickness, my weight ballooned. I weighed 170 pounds when it was time to deliver. I was huge all over, as wide as I was tall, and probably a pretty funny sight. But even so, I worked right up until the end of the eighth month doing shows.

Juli was born on January 25. About four o'clock that afternoon, Richard and I drove over to his parents' house. I was sitting on a low cabinet in their kitchen, chatting, when I noticed I had a stomachache. I had one real sharp pain and I said, "Oh, gosh, that hurt." Then I had another one about five minutes later and they said, "That's it." So Richard and I went home, gathered a few things together, and left Christi with my mother, who had flown down from Portland. By that time my pains were coming very quickly. I had my first pain at about 5:00 P.M. and at 8:45 that same night, Juli was born. It was a very quick delivery but a difficult one. During delivery my tailbone was broken, a nerve was pinched, and my bladder was injured.

Oral came and prayed for me and God healed my tailbone, but I was still in great pain from the pinched nerve and having trouble with my bladder. My doctor kept telling me that my bladder problems were all in my head, and Oral reassured me that having a baby was the most natural thing in the world.

"Come on, Patti," he teased me, "you know you're stronger than this." He was right; I'd never been sick and I certainly wasn't a whiny person, so I was stunned when the most natural thing in the world almost killed me!

After three days, Richard took me home from the hospital, but that night I became very weak and began to pass out. Richard called the doctor who agreed to meet us at his office. On the way I began hemorrhaging and lost a lot of blood. The doctor took one look at me and called an ambulance. They put me back in the hospital and immediately began looking for blood. I'm AB positive so they had to look all over Oklahoma to find enough but they finally were able to transfuse me sufficiently.

They gave me blood and antibiotics and started taking this "natural" phenomenon more seriously. I was there for another three weeks, during which time I lost forty pounds. They had to take me back to surgery to repair my bladder but I was just relieved that it really was a medical problem and not that I was crazy.

A month after I got home I was up and walking around when Oral came down with a terrible case of the flu. I went up to see him and he was lying in bed. I just peeked my head in and said, "Oral, it's the most natural thing in the world. You'll feel better in a minute." When he got well, he laughed, but he didn't think it was funny then.

After Juli's birth, we moved to another house. It had one more bedroom, a larger mortgage and a beautiful back yard. I got my first car—a station wagon, because I was a suburban housewife now. We hired our first nanny, a little old Danish grandmother named Karen. She took care of the children while Richard and I were working.

I bought Richard a blue Mercedes for Christmas and shortly after that I got my first Jaguar. We joined Southern Hills Country Club. We were now officially an important part of the dynasty, and later that year Richard was chosen to be head of the Oral Roberts Evangelistic Association.

Our life style changed drastically over the next three years. We went from living in a duplex and driving one old American car to owning an expensive home and driving foreign luxury cars; from buying local, ready-made, off-the-rack clothing to ordering the finest Italian suits, silk ties and hand-crafted leather accessories. We justified our increasingly lavish life styles because all of our efforts were directed toward building a Christian empire. We could go sing and in one weekend raise a million dollars to help build a university.

At first I was a little uneasy about the huge amounts of money that were made available to us and I occasionally questioned Richard about it. He always reminded me that the Bible said a workman was worthy of his hire, and that if the ox treads the grain he has a right to eat some of it.

After several years I stopped asking. I enjoyed the prerogatives of wealth as much as anyone and I took comfort in it. I stopped seeing the Oral Roberts Association as a primarily spiritual endeavor and began seeing it as a corporate one. I rationalized that I was the wife of the head of a major corporation and therefore we could live like the heads of other major corporations.

Between tapings for the TV show, we often took expensive and lengthy vacations and soon established a sort of "jet set" life style.

One of our favorite spots was Palm Beach. We stayed at the Breakers, a beautiful, elegant old hotel. During the day Richard golfed while the children and I swam and played; then we'd all rendezvous for dinner. Everyone would get all dressed up in suits and ties and long gowns, and we'd go to eat in the very formal hotel dining room.

The dining room had an orchestra that played every night. Richard and I didn't dance, but he would take the children out on the floor with him. They were so small he couldn't bend over and dance with them, so he just carried them in his arms and waltzed around the floor while they squealed with delight. They made a striking picture. Richard looked like a movie idol in his dark suit and the children looked like little cherubs. We always dressed them in frilly white dresses, all covered with lace, and both of them had naturally curly hair, so all you could see as they whirled around the floor were lots of curls and angelic-looking faces with pink cheeks and adoring eyes following their daddy.

At other times we'd fly out to Palm Springs and rent a house with some friends for a week or two. We'd get up early to avoid the heat of the day, and the men would go play golf while the women swam or played with the children, or shopped. At night we'd all go out to eat. We usually ended up at the Hungry Tiger, which the children loved because it had live lobsters that swam around in a tank and they thought that was terrific.

After dinner we'd play cards or Monopoly and listen to music until late into the night. Then we'd get up and start the whole process over again. One lazy, long, sun-filled day stretched into another until it was time to go home and start work again.

It was a lovely way to live but totally unreal. We lived like characters in a novel or a made-for-TV movie about the beautiful people and I reveled in it. Having made a truce, albeit an uneasy one, with my conscience over the source of our wealth, I proceeded to enjoy its prerogatives with total abandon.

Richard and I were comfortable with each other then, but our lives were becoming increasingly remote and I was becoming increasingly unhappy about our relationship. It was the one dark cloud in an otherwise silverplated life.

Richard and I looked married. We acted married. We did all the things that other married couples did, but we fell far short of the biblical ideal of being one. We were roommates and stage partners. Our communication problems had increased until now there was very little genuine communication between us. We were polite and considerate to each other, and we sincerely tried to please each other, but we were not lovers, husband and wife, nurtured by each other, cared for and protected. Those words were not part of our marriage.

Being the romantic that I am, the occasional realization of our situation always sent me into a depression. For a week I would mope around the house, cry, and in general make life miserable for everyone. Richard was always very solicitous at those times, but since they were short-lived, he attributed them to overwork or female moodiness. It didn't occur to him that they might be symptoms of something deeper.

Richard took a more typically male approach to our difficulties. We might not be ecstatically happy, but as long as we weren't fighting and the externals of our life ran smoothly, he couldn't believe that we might have serious problems. I couldn't make him understand the disaster I saw looming ahead of us if something in our relationship didn't change.

So we continued to live in our fantasy world—filling up the empty places in our hearts with expensive clothes, cars, vacations, and work. Our money enabled us to buy separation, to get away and not face the growing difficulties in our lives. By the time we would finally be forced to face them, it would be too late.

CHAPTER SEVEN

No Success
without a Successor

In the center of our bedroom stood a beautiful old bed with a heavily carved headboard that went clear to the ceiling. Oral had given us the bed. Often when I looked at it, I thought how appropriate that was since he was at the center of our lives. We slept in his bed and, in many ways, he slept in ours.

Oral was the fixed point in our changing lives. He was our frame of reference. Everything we did revolved around him and the ministry. Our marriage was a triangle with Oral at the tip.

From the day that I had first set foot on the ORU campus, I had had a love/hate relationship with Oral. Now, both my love and my hate for him were intensified. I still loved him for the dream and the call of God that was so obviously on his life, but I began to hate what I thought he was doing to Richard.

It was becoming more and more apparent now that the only option Richard thought he had anymore was to become Oral, Jr. He would take his father's sermons out of the archives, study them, and then go preach them verbatim. That angered me because I knew that Richard was bright enough to make up his own sermons. He didn't need to become a clone of his father. I could respect Richard, but I didn't like the carbon copy of Oral I saw emerging.

I realize now that this was a critical period in Richard's professional life. He was still insecure and unsure of exactly where he fit in the ministry. Preaching Oral's sermons grew more out of his fears and uncertainties than out of a conscious attempt to recreate himself in Oral's image. Had I been more sensitive and more spiritually mature, I might have realized that and responded to Richard with compassion and support instead of contempt.

As it was, I grieved over what I perceived as Richard's loss of identity. Everything that he had been afraid would happen if he joined his father's ministry seemed to be occurring, and I felt partly responsible. What frustrated me even more was that Richard seemed unaware of the transformation that was taking place. I began to feel that Richard was being sacrificed for Oral's dream and that he was intoxicated by the power and wealth that were showered on us. He seemed to be willingly crawling up on the altar. One night, about a year after Richard had become head of the Evangelistic Association, I poured out my grief and frustration in my diary.

"Richard doesn't see what's happening to him," I wrote. "It's almost as if he has been anesthetized and they were cutting off his legs and saying, 'We're going to give these legs to God, Richard. These legs are anointed. We're going to build something on them.' And then his arms. And all the while Oral is saying, 'Richard, it's wonderful to have you in the ministry and to see God working in your life like this. It's just awesome. You're so anointed. You're really called to take *my* place, to take up where *I* left off, to finish *my* dream.'

"What about the voice of God in Richard's life? Doesn't anybody care about that? Doesn't anybody cry at night saying, 'What about Richard?' Does he have a chance to hear God in his own life without hearing him through Oral's mouth?''

I was frightened for Richard and for us. Oral always said that success without a successor was failure, and I began to feel that we were being recreated in his image. We were to be the second generation Oral and Evelyn. Richard wasn't Richard; he was Oral with another name—Oral at age twenty-five again. But, unfortunately, I wasn't Evelyn, and therein lay a large part of the problem. Once, after Oral and I had gotten into one of our arguments, Evelyn said to me, "Why can't you be more like me instead of like Oral? And why can't Richard be like Oral instead of like me?" That would have made things a lot simpler. But even though I loved Evelyn, I didn't want to *be* her. I wanted to be Patti, and I wanted Richard to be Richard.

Oral sensed my apprehension and he began to warn Richard about me. "If you don't get her under control, she's going to do to you like Granny did to Papa." He built a fear into Richard that he would end up like Oral's father—seemingly insignificant and unremembered, eclipsed by a woman.

Oral's mother was an incredibly strong woman. She possessed great faith and spiritual authority along with a very domineering personality. By all I can figure out from the stories told about her, she had almost emasculated Oral's father. Oral's own personality was strong enough that she had not been able to control him, but she had injured him enough so that he had a supreme distrust of women. The stronger and more vibrant personality they had, the more suspect they were. In his eyes, any woman who combined a powerful, charismatic personality with a love for God was "Granny."

When he told Richard I was like Granny, he was not

speaking with endearment about his mother. He was saying, "She's dangerous; watch out for her." I was reaping the fruit of Oral's terror of his mother. And I alarmed him because I quite possibly could alter his plans for Richard.

Once in one of our more heated discussions, I remember him saying to me, "I did not build this university or this ministry for you. I built it for Richard. You will never get to the top. It's not yours; it's Richard's." I can only think that Oral had a fear that I eventually would dominate Richard and therefore frustrate his overall design.

Had I not married Richard, I think Oral and I would have gotten along famously because, in spite of our conflicts, we were really very much alike, as Evelyn had noted. The things I resented in Oral, I resented because I knew I had the same potential. We are both very straightforward people and have a tendency, if we are not held in check, to become abusive and manipulative of people.

Even during our worst times, there was a part of me that wanted to please Oral, because I still had great respect for him and there is a side of him that I love very much. If he hadn't taken himself so seriously and the people around him hadn't taken him so seriously, he could probably be king of the world because he has such a loving, charming personality.

There is a lot of God in Oral, a lot of creativity. He's a wonderful, wonderful person. I think he's genuinely wonderful, not solely wonderful in the way that everyone thinks—as a great preacher or founder of a university. Certainly those things are admirable, but he's delightful in areas that he doesn't know about. He is disarming when, like a shy little boy, he does things to make you notice him. He becomes so childlike that one cannot help giving in and wildly applauding his efforts. I particularly loved it when he would try to tell a joke. He always messed up but the show he put on was much funnier than the joke could ever have been.

He's not, however, a particularly warm person. It's hard for him to be real cuddly and affectionate. I can't remember him ever kissing me on the cheek. Usually, instead of hugging me, he would just slap me on the back.

The incongruities of this highly complex man are often rather fetching. For instance, he has very simple tastes— that is, until it gets to hardware. He doesn't care if he has butter beans or filet mignon, but he likes a good jet, and I always found that to be a good, manly characteristic. Also, the same man who has read, reread, and loved every Louis L'Amour novel ever written also reads with effortless comprehensive power the writings of Nietzsche and Bonhoeffer.

He's very careful about reading the news and he knows what's happening in the world. He is a very bright, perceptive man. He's probably not a genius, but he has a charismatic personality, coupled with intelligence, a handsome face, and personal charm, and there isn't anything he couldn't do. A lot of people have told him he'd make a great politician, and they're right. He already *is* a great politician. He could have been a great elected official. But he was smart enough to know he could have it all without going to the trouble of being elected.

Oral is not overly impressed by government officials. He respects people like Billy Graham or the late Kathryn Kuhlman more than even the president. He might be flattered by the attention of a president because it would reinforce his belief that he was important, but he wouldn't, in his heart of hearts, consider him his peer.

He could only consider those his peers who had ultimate power, and the ultimate power is spiritual power.

For all of his achievements, Oral still evidences a great, underlying insecurity that is often found in those who grew up in poverty. He has a haunting fear of being poor, which, when you think it through, could be the springboard for his Seed-Faith theology. I don't believe that a middle-class Presbyterian child who had a nice red bicycle, who grew up knowing he was going to go to college, knowing he was eventually going to get a middle- to high-income job, would ever preach the prosperity message so long and so faithfully as Oral has.

The most important thing in the world to Oral is his ministry. He is possessed by a sense of destiny. As Wayne Robinson noted in his biography, *Oral*, the one thing that Oral believes more than anything else, as much as he believes the Bible or the creeds of the church, is that he has been called of God "to bring healing to my generation." *Nothing* comes before his ministry—not his wife, his children, or anyone or anything else. Just how important the ministry is to him is apparent from a statement he made at the height of the City of Faith controversy. Speaking to a group of local businessmen in Tulsa, he stated that if he did not finish the City of Faith, he was in danger of losing his soul. Now I know Oral well enough to know that he did not mean by that that he would literally lose his salvation and go to hell, but his soul—everything he believes in, everything he has hoped and dreamed and worked and suffered for. His life itself is so inextricably bound up with the ministry that the two have become inseparable. He will sacrifice anything for it.

The thing he hates most is disloyalty. He considers differences of opinion as infidelity. That was always a mysterious part of his character to me, because he genuinely respects honest dissent. But insecurity seems to cause him to characterize it as disloyalty.

I always thought it sad that the people around him didn't realize the respect he had for intelligent dissent. If they had, they might have risked it more, and they might have been more help to Oral in the long run.

Evelyn is actually the perfect mate for a man such as Oral. She is a woman of great faith and of great courage. While he crisscrossed the globe bringing the message of God's healing power to millions of strangers, she raised their four children alone. She was a devoted mother, but Oral's frequent absences played havoc with their family and drove a wedge between Oral and his children which is still not entirely healed.

Unlike Evelyn, I was not willing to place the ministry above my family, shredded as it was. That brought me into inevitable ideological conflict with Oral.

For Richard, who was caught in the middle, it must have seemed like an impossible situation. Since he had never, in the larger sense, left his father to cleave to his wife, when the two came in conflict, he was faced with a very painful dilemma.

To his credit, Richard at times defended me. On one occasion when Oral and I disagreed, Richard sided with me, but Oral refused to back down or to forgive me for disagreeing with him. Richard got Oral on the half-hour show and read him a Scripture which said in effect that a man who does not have forgiveness in his heart cannot know God. Oral was visibly moved and told Richard he had given him a lot to think about. The two of them then held hands and prayed together, and it turned out to be a good show.

I think Richard sincerely wanted the marriage to work.

He wanted to make me happy but he didn't know how. He had no frame of reference and no role model, and we received no help. We traveled the globe and had contacts with almost every major ministry in the world, but our interior world was very narrowly circumscribed. We lived in a large house on a hill surrounded by twenty-four-hour guards and protected by an electronic gate. The guards kept intruders out, but in a very real sense they also kept us in. Our entire world centered in the Oral Roberts Association. We were insulated from outside influences that could have given us a fresh, biblically objective perspective on our problems.

I felt as if I was sixteen years old again, fighting my father for the chance to go to ORU. Only this time the stakes were much higher. I was fighting not just for myself but for Richard and for our family. I wanted him to make the same kind of emotional and psychological break from his father that I had made from mine. I wanted both of us to have a chance to be ourselves, to discover who we could be in God.

I still believe that my basic perceptions were right, but my attitude was totally wrong. When I felt that the ministry, and particularly Oral, threatened our marriage, I became very frightened and then very angry. Instead of supporting Richard and encouraging him to develop his own gifts, I tried to force him to break with his father. And instead of waging my battles where they would have done the most good, in my prayer closet, I waged them against those people who threatened me. It was a strategy born out of desperation, and it was destined to lose. I was defeated almost before I began. The final outcome might still have been the same, but I'll never know.

CHAPTER EIGHT

On Collision Course

Several years ago Peter Sellers played the role of Chauncy Gardner in a movie called *Being There*. Chauncy was an illiterate gardener whose only knowledge of the world came from television. His total immersion in the world of TV had left him passive, unaware, with no notion of himself, his life, or others. He was the ultimate media creation. He was, also, in this rather dark comedy, a huge success. Emerging from the walled garden he had cultivated all his life, he became a presidential advisor, a media pundit, and finally presidential timber himself. Success came to him because he reflected on everyone he met whatever qualities they projected on him.

In many ways, the last three years of our marriage resembled Chauncy's life. It is not straining the analogy to say that the marriage we showed on TV was the only one we had. It, too, was a media creation and a good one. But it had little life of its own apart from the television show. We successfully projected to our audience the image of the happily married couple that they wanted to see.

Just how true this was was forcefully brought home to me one day when Richard and I were invited to sing at a concert. There were a number of other Christian celebrities on the program and we all had to stay at the rehearsal hall for most of the day. While Richard and I waited for our turn to rehearse, we sat together in the darkened auditorium for five hours and never once spoke or looked at each other. Then we got up on stage and sang, holding hands and looking like the perfect married couple.

But the strain of living a lie began to take its toll on us. We were both miserable, but neither of us knew what to do about it. What made it even more frustrating was that no one in our family or our organization seemed to think that anything was wrong. They all acted as if our situation was normal. I think now that they were probably as frightened and confused as we were. They didn't know what to do to help us so they just joined in the deception, trying to pretend, as were we, that everything was all right. But, at the time, I interpreted their silence as approval. I began to wonder if there was something wrong with me. I decided that I must not be spiritual enough or certainly I would not be so unhappy.

So, I embarked on a concerted campaign to become the kind of wife I thought Richard wanted and the Bible required. I fought determinedly to crucify my old selfish, willful self and I started keeping a diary in which I recorded my struggle. One entry made after Richard and I had disagreed over the choice of music for one of the TV shows illustrated how confused and desperate I was.

I have been praying to know the complete and true meaning of dying to myself and picking up the cross. I have been praying also that God would use Richard to help me die. He is the hardest person to die in front of. In fact, in the past, I have found it much more expedient not to give in, not to die to my wishes and to bow to God's.

But God answers my prayers. He has begun a purifying project in my life. I had deep trouble with Richard about the music for the half-hour shows. I haven't fully given in to his wishes before because I don't trust his understanding of the whole situation. With God's help I was able to relinquish my rights and to try to act godly—to die. It hurt so much, but it had to be done, especially since God reminded me of my desire to grow spiritually.

An interesting thing happened to remind me. After Richard's and my discussion of music, my heart was full of disgust and distaste, bitterness and frustration—all things I've been trying to release to the cleansing blood of Jesus. I went to my room and a funny thing happened: the light over my bed was flickering, the light over my sink was flickering, the light in my closet was flickering. All the other lights were steady except for mine. I felt God was showing me that that was my testimony. My commitment to Him was flickering. My sins of hate were blocking out God's will for my life. My lights were flickering. After a prayer of confession and a good talk with the Lord, I felt restored. Incidentally, all the lights came on!

It's difficult to describe the war that raged inside me. I kept thinking, "It's me. I'm just not pure enough. I'm not Christian enough. I've got to die."

I read every book I could find on how to build a happy marriage. I tried to be the Total Woman, but all my efforts only left me nervous, exhausted, depressed, and no closer to my husband than before.

For the first time in our marriage we began to have terrible fights. I would lash out at him, accusing him of putting his father ahead of me and the children.

"All you care about is pleasing your father," I'd scream at him. "I am just a prop in your life. I don't really have a place in your heart."

"What do you expect from me, Patti?" he'd cry. "You know I care about you and the girls but God has called me to Dad's ministry and if I ever leave it He'll destroy me."

Every time we had these blowups, we'd end them by falling into each other's arms in tears. We'd sit on our bed and weep, calling out to God, begging Him to help us and promising that we would do better. We would pray together and have family devotions. Strangely, at those times I felt safe Just hearing Richard cry, knowing that he hated our situation as much as I did, made me feel protected and loved. For a few days I felt hope, but then we would get back to the sheer, ongoing business of the ministry. We had to do shows and make appearances and be Richard and Patti Roberts.

Things seemed so hopeless now that we finally decided to seek some outside counseling. We went to see Dr. L. D. Thomas of the First Methodist Church in Tulsa. Dr. Thomas was a wise and compassionate counselor, and had we continued to see him, he probably would have helped us, but we quit going after two sessions. It was obvious from those sessions that there were no quick, easy solutions to our problems, and we weren't ready to face the painful decisions we would have to make to repair the marriage. But Dr. Thomas's counsel did relieve the pressure enough to allow us to function for a few more months.

After our attempts at counseling with Dr. Thomas failed, I became increasingly despondent. In desperation during this time, I decided to visit Kathryn Kuhlman. She was holding a service in St. Louis, and I called and asked if I could come and talk to her. I was a little afraid to meet her; yet there was such stress in our lives, and I couldn't think of anybody I could talk to about it.

I didn't really know much about Kathryn. I didn't know she had been married and that it had been a failed marriage. I just felt instinctively that she would understand, and I knew she didn't have anything to gain by spreading rumors about the Roberts family, so I felt safe in confiding in her.

She was staying in a very elegant hotel in St. Louis. There was a flower shop in the lobby, and I stopped and bought her two dozen Sonia roses which the florist put in a big crystal vase. I arrived at her room roses on arm and heart in hand.

She greeted me at the door herself. She was wearing a midcalf navy blue dress, very elegant and very ladylike. She had on black suede sandals that wrapped at the ankle and big loop earrings, topped by this bushy red hair. "My goodness," I thought, "she's the most outrageous figure I've ever seen!"

The room was filled with flowers and boxes of candy, expressions of love that people had given her. Later I discovered that wherever she went people treated her that way.

Five minutes after our initial greeting, we were both sitting on the floor and the great spiritual leader had gone off and we were enjoying girl talk, just chatting and giggling. It was wonderful, and I fell in love with her immediately. She had such a zest for life, and everything was so interesting to her. She had been wondering what had been happening with the Robertses and she questioned me about every member of the family.

She kept asking, "When is Oral going to get back to preaching?" She believed he'd laid aside his primary calling, preaching and praying for the sick, in preference for the university. She had no ill feelings about the university. She thought it was a wonderful thing and should be done, but not at the expense of his primary ministry.

It was just like talking to some chatty columnist. We sat there on the floor and cried and laughed. It was hardly what I had expected from the great Kathryn Kuhlman. We'd look at a problem in my life and she would just rear back her head and laugh at the idiocy of the situation.

She was the first person who suggested to me that maybe Richard and I didn't have the capacity to be emotionally or spiritually intimate, that maybe because of the traumas of his childhood he had closed off that part of his life. Perhaps his heart of hearts was trapped inside a wall and he couldn't get out.

I had never considered that about Richard or me. I just thought he was unwilling to communicate and that he wouldn't let me inside where he lived. And I, because of my intense need for feedback, interaction, and reassurance, just stood outside the walls and pummeled them first with pleas for Richard to come out, then with threats, and then with emotional battering rams. I always felt as much of a stranger to Richard Roberts as strangers and employees did. I lived with him and people would ask me, "What's he really like?" and I'd say, "I don't know what he's like. I wish I knew. I wish I had some way to feel like I belong to him and he belongs to me, some handle to get in." I could never get in. I could never figure out what was going on inside there. It was as if Oral and Evelyn held the key to the real Richard Roberts and I couldn't get in and they couldn't or wouldn't give me the key.

Dino Kartsonakis, Kathryn's keyboard artist, was staying down the hall. About noon he knocked on the door. Kathryn and I had forgotten the time, so the three of us went out to a little restaurant down the street. Over lunch we decided that we should get on an old bus (à la Vintage Quartet style) and go on tour. Forget about all evangelistic associations, TV shows, and crusades—just drive around the country and hold little services and have fun. It was a lovely, funny idea and we laughed about it all afternoon.

Kathryn was not afraid to be a person. She didn't have a personality that could be defined or limited to religion—as in rigidly pious. She was natural and there was nothing bent up about her. She was a joy to be with. Of course, she could be very painful to be around. But even then, she was human. She didn't hide her humanity behind a mask of spirituality. I think that was what kept Kathryn pure. That's what allowed her to have great amounts of money and fame without being totally destroyed by them. She was a straight shooter and I loved that in her, and I began to be angry at the contrast I was coming to see back in our own camp.

That night I went to her service and wept at the tremendous love God expressed through her. And not all of it came from her. At times during the meetings, it seemed as if clouds of love would fall on the people.

That was very new to me, because we didn't operate that way. By comparison, our meetings seemed forced. Hers had a spontaneity that we didn't have. We arrived a few minutes before the meeting started, ministered well-rehearsed songs and sermons, then stepped quickly into a waiting limousine as soon as the service was over.

I left Kathryn Kuhlman the next day and my life was changed. She made me feel less guilty for being unable to communicate with Richard, and she helped me to put my marriage problems into better perspective. That didn't solve anything, but at least it relieved me of an enormous burden of guilt and gave me some tools of understanding to work with.

After that, Kathryn kind of adopted me, and I would often fly out to her meetings at the Shrine Auditorium in California. On one of those trips Richard came with me, and after that we were almost always a threesome. Kathryn found him so charming and delightful, and he treated her with such love and respect, they developed a beautiful friendship.

Once after the three of us had become friends, Richard and I went to California to have dinner with her. We flew out, rented a car, and threw our suitcases in the back seat. Halfway between the airport and Bel Air, where we were to meet her, we realized that we needed to change out of our jeans and that we would not have time to go to our hotel before we met Kathryn. We pulled off on a side road, pulled our clothes out, and began changing. While Richard watched for trucks coming by, I slipped into a black cashmere Halston dress, pulled on my panty hose and slippers, and found my jewelry. Then while I watched the traffic, he changed into a beautiful suit, and we met Kathryn on time, if a little disheveled, at the Bel Air Country Club.

Before she met Richard, Kathryn wouldn't have given me two cents for our marriage, but afterwards she had a lot more hope. Kathryn prayed and wept with both of us, both individually and together. She didn't solve anything for us, but her love was so great it made us want to try. We knew she didn't want us to stay together "for the sake of the ministry," although she would always pray, "Jesus, you know we wouldn't do anything to blacken your name," and it was a cry from her soul. She was a precious gift in our lives, not because of her great marital counseling but because of her love. When she died, it was a tremendous loss to us personally and to our marriage. There was no condemnation in Kathryn's approach to us. Her empathy and concern were real. Neither of us was of any particular use to her. I suppose she loved us only for what we were, not for any potential that we might possess. Being with her was a treat for both of us—we giggled, laughed, and played, and we enjoyed her radiant attention. We soaked up her unbiased love because it was the first unconditional love either of us had ever known.

Kathryn's love gave us a brief respite from the wretched problems we faced. She had been a mediator, a welcomed truce-maker for two tired fighters. But the old injuries quickly flared up again. When we were with her we could relax and lower our walls just a little. We not only laughed with her, but we could cry, and that was a great release as well as a treasured gift. In her protective company it was safe to do something so nakedly human as to cry. When you can weep, you can lament the loss, lament the agony, and there's a chance. But after Kathryn left, the tears were scarce. The gulf between Richard and me was so great, the presence of love was so absent, when the tears were gone so was the last thread of hope for the marriage.

During this time I can remember coming into the house and finding Richard in the den listening to the Gaither-Huff *Alleluia* album with his head in his hands, tears seeping between his fingers. Later, after he had left, I would go into the den, sit in the same chair, put *Alleluia* on the stereo and do exactly as he had done. That record ministered greatly to both of us, but we could never listen to it together. There were millions of miles between us that we seemingly couldn't cross over to get to each other's hearts.

In November 1976, several months after Kathryn died, Richard and I were invited to sing at the Praise Gathering for Believers Concert in Indianapolis We were having serious problems by this time, and it was an effort to conceal our hostility during the long rehearsal that preceded the concert.

When it was finally over, we got into our rented car and drove back to our hotel, the Indianapolis Hilton. After finding a parking space close to the back door of the underground garage, Richard pulled the key out of the ignition, turned to me, and said, "Patti, this is not working out. I'm not happy, you're not happy. I want you to leave. Just take your things and get out."

The reflection from the red exit light over the door cast a pinkish glow in the half-lit parking lot. I stared at him and said nothing. Anger, a great and terrible rage, welled up inside me. I wanted to scream, to lash out at him and say, "How dare you? You can't kick me out of your life. Who do you think you are? You talk about being the great Oral Roberts's son and you can't even make a family for yourself." But I didn't.

I had such contempt for him at that moment that there were not words in the language strong enough to express my feelings. I would not have given him the satisfaction of knowing that he had upset me. I turned to him and said quietly, "Richard, I'm not leaving." Then I got out of the car and went up to our room to get ready for the evening's performance. Richard followed a few minutes later, and neither of us spoke again until we got to the concert hall.

We performed that night without displaying even a trace of the rancor and supreme disgust we were feeling for each other. Anyone watching us would have seen only two people who looked very much in love.

After the concert, I wandered aimlessly through the booths that had been set up in the lobby to display Christian books and records. I noticed an interesting-looking young man sitting behind one of the book tables. He had a different air about him—like a prophet about to speak out—so I stopped and picked up one of the books at his table, *How Shall We Then Live?* I had never heard of its author, Francis Schaeffer, or his son, Franky Schaeffer V, who was manning the booth. But as I started talking with him I discovered that he was angry, too. We were both angry with the superstar system of American religion. I told Franky about the problems that Richard and I were having and asked if he could help us. He agreed to try if Richard was willing. So the next afternoon the three of us gathered in one of the Hilton's conference rooms.

Richard and I took turns spilling out our feelings. I said, "I feel like Richard ignores me and I feel like Oral thinks I'm some sort of threat. But I don't know why. I just want to be loved and accepted but they won't do it unless I play according to their terms. If I play the role, then they'll like me, and if I don't, they won't."

Richard said basically the same thing about me to Franky. "If she'll just stop fighting me and fit in with the ministry, everything will be okay."

I think Franky thought we were both pretty fouled up but predictable products of the high-gloss religious atmosphere where the appearance of holiness is more important than relationships. He questioned us closely about our family relationships. "Do you play with your family? Do you go on retreats that are just family? What kind of quality time are you investing in each other's lives—not in behalf of the ministry but in behalf of Richard and Patti?"

He asked Richard, "What are you giving to Patti of yourself? Not your money, not a charge account at

Giorgio's or an open account at Neiman-Marcus—what are you giving of *you* to Patti Roberts?"

Then he asked me the same kind of questions. "Patti, what are you giving to Richard? Are you giving him love and support and devotion? Do you respond to him as your husband or as your co-worker on stage in the Oral Roberts ministry?"

I didn't answer. I wasn't ready to say, "I respond to him as a co-worker." I didn't know how to respond to Richard as a husband according to Franky's definition. I'd never had him as that kind of a husband. I'd never known him apart from the ministry except for the first two months we were married.

Franky told Richard that there would never be any chance in our marriage until he preferred me over his work and decided to cherish me as his wife.

Richard didn't say to Franky, "I don't love her," but Richard's definition of love was different from Franky's. Richard felt that he demonstrated his love by taking care of me and seeing that I got what I wanted, but Franky kept pressing home the point that what I really wanted was not Richard's possessions, but Richard. But I'd grown so cold that I didn't particularly want either.

Franky suggested that we come to L'Abri, the Schaeffers' counseling center in Switzerland, but we never did. Our lives went at such a fast pace and we were professionally so busy being us that to take the time to go to Switzerland for counseling would have been out of the question.

I know now that Franky was right. To have fixed our marriage we would have had to have temporarily left the show and sought extensive counseling, but that was just too costly. Neither Richard nor I had the faith or the courage to take such a drastic step.

So we survived by repressing our problems—by pushing them away from us. We spun a silky web of fantasy around our lives, but we both knew we would have to face the truth sooner or later. We could not continue to lie to ourselves and the public forever. We were moving swiftly toward a head-on collision with reality.

CHAPTER NINE

The Race to Endure

In 1976 Richard and I and the World Action Singers developed a concert program saluting the first two hundred years of American music. Ralph Carmichael had arranged for us this lively bicentennial tribute to American composers, and we performed it everywhere we traveled that year.

One of my numbers was a song entitled "She's Only a Bird in a Gilded Cage." I carried a large basket on stage with me, and as I sang I tossed small stuffed birds into the audience. The birds grew larger and more ornate until, at the song's climax, I pulled out a large rubber chicken, grasped it by the neck and shook it, all the while maintaining a perfectly straight face. The audience loved it and it never failed to get a hearty laugh. But I had difficulty fully enjoying the humor in it. It was too true. I felt that not only was I imprisoned in the gilded cage, but we all were.

We lived luxurious, storybook lives, but all of our acquisitions and acclaim still left us very lonely and tired and spiritually hungry. We had built a wonderful machine in the name of God, and now all of our efforts were focused on keeping it running. At all costs, it must never be allowed to stop. So, the masters eventually became the slaves and the machine that we had created now controlled us.

We had erected a beautiful spiritual edifice, but behind it there seemed to be nothing but emptiness and chaos. A religious exterior without the softening humility of the Holy Spirit operating in and through the person inside creates a tremendous void.

As members of one of America's foremost Christian empires, we were allowed great personal excesses. None of us were having affairs, or siphoning off funds from the ministry, but we wallowed in spiritual indifference and pride. The ministry that had been founded to serve the needs of the people, separated us from the people, and also from anyone who might have had the insight or the spiritual authority to call us to task for our sins of pride.

To raise the enormous amount of money he needed just to keep the day-to-day operation of the Evangelical Association and the university running smoothly, Oral had to develop contacts among leaders in the government and business community. It was a fact of life that he could tap more financial and political capital for the ministry during one golf game at the Southern Hills Country Club than he could in a week of Partners' meetings. However, in order to be accepted by those who possess wealth and influence, one has to adopt at least some of the trappings of their life style and that inevitably creates conflicts.

Jesus said we were to be servants, but it is hard to maintain a servant's heart when you dress better than some heads of state and live better than 99 percent of the world. When you play golf with senators and vacation with heads of multimillion-dollar corporations, it is difficult to identify with the widow on Social Security who faithfully supports the ministry with her ten-dollar offering each month. The weight of success tends to remove you from the reality of the Spirit of God—from the bleeding, wounded, compassionate heart of Jesus. I have no distaste for wealth, country clubs, senators, or golf games. The problem I had was more one of balance. It's the age-old problem of how to be in the world but not of it.

We became so blinded to our own excesses that we saw nothing incongruous about singing before a Partners' meeting to raise millions of dollars for a new building, then toasting the success of our efforts with a lavish night out on the town.

The use of television as our primary means of ministry created a paradox and a problem for us. While television enabled us to reach more people, it also allowed us to remain very remote. Public meetings and concerts bring you into direct contact with hurting, needy people. Television insulates you from them. You tape the shows and by the time they air, you are in Palm Springs vacationing. Volunteer counselors man the telephone hotlines and computers sort, open, and answer the mail. Television also confers tremendous power and wealth on its stars whether they are religious or secular, and that is perhaps its greatest attraction as well as its greatest danger.

Power corrupts. She is a seductive mistress and many men who would never dream of being immoral or dishonest have fallen prey to her charms. Religious power is usually more subtle, but it is no less devastating.

It is easy to elevate those who minister on television or in concerts or through books to a more spiritual plane than "ordinary" Christians, to assume that they have none of the foibles and failures that the rest of us grapple with as human beings. We seem to have a perverse tendency to want to create idols. Whether they are golden calves or Christian superstars, idols are simple and certainly less threatening to deal with than the living God. It is easy for us to fall into embracing what Richard Foster calls "the religion of the mediator." If we are not very careful, we can move quickly and totally unconsciously into worshiping God's servants instead of God. But no man or woman can stand the weight of worship. It is intoxicating and highly addictive. It perverts one's way of thinking and bends one's personality. The load is too much. You lose sight of who you are in God and you're pressed to believe your own publicity, which is exactly what happened to us.

None of us were evil people. We truly loved God and wanted to serve Him. We never sat down and said, "We are going to become arrogant, calloused, and insensitive." These maladies slip up on people. No one loved us enough to hold us accountable. No one looked beneath the glitter to see if our lives matched our performance. No one, except perhaps Franky Schaeffer V, ever questioned our value system. As long as we were successful, we were accepted uncritically.

I think a certain segment of the Christian community has developed a whole new twist on the fruits today. In our success-saturated culture, the fruits of the Spirit, the fruits of a godly life, often seem less appealing than the fruits of success. Now, instead of looking for the marks of the Spirit in a person's life—love, joy, peace, long-suffering, and the others, we have a tendency to consider the cars he drives, the clothes he wears, or the buildings he's built as the measure of God's grace in his life and the quality of his relationship to God.

I know a lot of people were blessed and sincerely ministered to by what we sang on TV, and by what we said—but the overall picture, I'm afraid, seemed to say, "If you follow our formula, you'll be like us," rather than, "If you do what Jesus says, you'll be like Him." It was certainly more exciting to follow us, because to follow us was to identify with success, with glamour, with a theology that made everything good and clean and well-knit together. To identify with Jesus, however, meant to identify with the Cross.

I believe we gave people a lesser explanation of the Gospel and we lived by a lesser explanation. We lived very true to our mentality, and we bore the consequences of living true to it. I'm always a little bemused when people say to me, "What happened to your marriage? Did the devil just attack you all of a sudden?" No, the devil didn't attack us suddenly. Our divorce was a direct result of the lives we lived.

Our success, our high-gloss way of living, our highly polished exterior gave us no refuge when the terrors of real problems hit, because our hope was in our empire. Our desire was to protect our empire. So all of our effort went to "how does this look to the public?"—not "how does this look to God?" We turned our eyes to the public when we should have turned them to the wind and cried, "God, what responsibilities do we have to You?"

By now, I had despaired of things ever improving. The situation was intolerable and I could not see any way out. Divorce was not in our vocabulary at that point, so I began praying to die. That was the only honorable escape as far as I could see. I became terribly cold and indifferent toward Richard. I was polite, but totally indifferent. I treated him cruelly by withholding the one thing he needed the most—my respect. I had nothing but contempt for him, and I made no effort to hide my feelings.

Richard had almost reached the end of his rope also. Things stood at an impasse between us. We were just waiting to see who would crack first. It is incredible to me now that two Christians could treat each other that way.

I am appalled by the way we acted. We no longer made any effort to repair our marriage. The race to endure was on.

At this point, I am not even sure that marital counseling would have helped us. It would have to have been intense and prolonged. I am convinced that there comes a point in any unhappy marriage where there is so much accumulated bitterness and hurt and mutual distrust that, barring a miracle, it cannot be healed. Of course, God can and does work miracles, but we didn't have the faith or even the desire to receive one any more. Richard and I had both reached the point where we were no longer able to seek wholeness.

We were both suffering, but we were not suffering for the sake of the Cross, fulfilling our biblical responsibilities toward each other in faith and hope that God would work a miracle in our lives. We were stoically enduring a bad marriage, just avoiding the embarrassment of getting a divorce.

Tragically, there are many Christians today, including some spiritual leaders, who are doing the same thing.

As I travel around the country, singing in churches, I am frequently approached by Christians of all stripes—pastors, celebrities, and ordinary parishioners—who pour out their hearts to me. They think that because I have experienced the trauma of a bad marriage and survived, that I am safe to confide in. Often they are desperate, hurt, crushed people, grasping at their last straw. They see some personal disaster marching relentlessly towards them but they haven't any idea what to do. They are terrified and are looking to me for legal loopholes, some justification for escaping from an unbearable situation.

It is not unusual for me to receive a phone call in the

middle of the night from a well-known Christian and hear him say, "I am living in hell, but I can't do anything about it because I'll let the cat out of the bag if I admit it. And I've got to keep up my work; I've got to keep up my ministry. It would present a fragmented front to the public if I sought counseling. Besides, I'd be too embarrassed to talk to a counselor. Everyone expects me to have my life together."

Sadly, these people often feel owned by, and responsible to, the ministry even more than they feel responsible to God. God forgives, but institutions do not. People can't take the time or the risk of seeking healing, because if the healing process in any way impinges on the operation of the institution, the institution immediately speaks out and demands loyalty. God is patient, longsuffering, and gentle. Institutions are not. Institutions scream louder than God and it is human nature to respond to that which speaks loudest and most insistently. So, rather than risk angering the institution, some Christians continue to live fragmented, destructive lives. But holding a marriage together for the sake of the ministry rather than the sanctity of their scriptural vows does not please God. God places tremendous importance on truth in human relationships, and when two people are living a lie in order to protect a ministry, they are violating God's definition of marriage.

God places incredible importance on love. He commands it. It is the first and the second "Thou shalt. . . ." God never makes love contingent on *feeling*. It is here that Christians have allowed themselves to be deceived by the world. To live in an unloving relationship is a tremendous failure in terms of following the Gospel. Simply enduring a bad marriage is not enough. The whole thrust of the New Testament is love, and if this is

violated at one of the most basic levels of human relationships, it has repercussions throughout the Body. Christians cannot talk about love to the world if they can't live
it, whether they *feel* like it or not, within the four walls of
their own home.

God designed marriage to be a nurturing place, a shelter. It is sandpaper on one side and silk on the other;
abrasive on one side and comforting on the other. It is the
test-kitchen of the gospel. It is a microcosm of God's plan
for the world. It is a little world of two people where
dying and resurrection take place and everything is
redeemed.

Marriage is not just a human convenience or a God-
sanctioned way of meeting the needs of the flesh or an
enjoyable way to populate the globe. To view it that way
is to miss the point entirely. Marriage is an oath to God
that with at least one other person in the world you will
see His kingdom realized. Nothing but death will stop
you from seeing the Cross and the Resurrection with all
its attendant glories manifested.

Marriage is a commitment that you will fight to see
your own and your mate's sicknesses healed, the scars
that life has inflicted on you both wiped away, and the
bent parts of your personalities straightened. It is a
pledge to work for redemption in each other's lives. That
is what Christ does for His Church. This is what He asks
us to do for each other.

For a Christian not to understand the significance of
marriage and to uphold the sanctity of it is to miss the
point of eternity.

The Christian marriage is meant to be a miniaturized,
made-for-just-two, identical replica of Christ and His
commitment to the Church. And that relationship—between Christ and His beloved—is the whole point of

human history. Time is allowed to exist only so that the bride can be made fully ready, beautified, tried and proven worthy of the great price that was paid for her. Then time will cease and the Lover and the beloved will be joined together forever.

The biblical parallels—Christ/husband and His bride/wife—are by no means accidental nor are they to be left as merely literary analogies. They are the keys to a greater truth. If Satan can attack the relationship between men and women in marriage, he can attack one of the most important laboratories for Christ's relationship to the Church. That is why it is so vital for the Church to understand the importance of the commitment involved in the sacrament of marriage.

It is one of Satan's foundational battle plans to keep these issues shrouded. If he can keep us locked into ego battles, simmering over women's rights versus men's rights, confused by tributary social issues, then he can keep us from pulling ourselves and our mates upright and seeing the grander issues. If I cannot bear true submission to my spouse and if he cannot reconcile himself to losing himself and all that he has for my benefit, how can we hope to actually bow in submission, loyalty, and love before Jesus. (I do not mean to imply that marriage is the *only* way to accomplish this. Certainly God can and does make provision for the single believer, but marriage is the norm for most people.)

Any person who places ministry above marriage has, at best, an incomplete understanding of the significance of marriage in God's eternal plans. When this flip-flop of priorities occurs it is a wonder that the skies don't thunder, "Let no man put asunder. . . ."

Divorce is a consequence of one of the biggest lies ever perpetrated on humanity. To divorce is to admit that something was more important than marriage. It is an act of treason. Granted, there are scriptural grounds for divorce. But largely, and certainly in our case, scriptural reasons couldn't be cited.

Many Christians have accepted the world's definition of love as a *feeling*. The Church did not counsel them that the euphoria would gradually diminish and how to cope when it did. Therefore instead of seeking Christian healing of their union, they seek new mates. And Satan will insure that there is always someone available to provide fresh "goose-pimple" feelings.

Divorce is an outgrowth of a sinful relationship between husbands and wives. And there are many piously married couples who are living divorced lives. They're divorced from reality, they're divorced from love, they're divorced from being knit together in a healthy, nourishing relationship. They're totally divorced. They live in a shell of a marriage with no content.

Richard and I were living in that state, but we refused to face the possibility of actual divorce. We deceived ourselves into thinking that we could continue indefinitely in that state. But other people had more insight than we. They knew what had been the real wedge that had cut into our union from the beginning, and they recognized that it would ultimately be stronger than our marriage vows. They were just waiting for the blowup and were already making plans to benefit from it. One man in the organization who had a lot to gain if Richard could be discredited was quietly urging him to go ahead and get a divorce.

One morning early in 1976 Rona Barrett broke the news on television that "Patti and Richard Roberts are rumored to be seeking a divorce." I was furious at the report because I felt it had been leaked from inside the organization to damage Richard's credibility. But I couldn't do anything about it. There was just enough truth to it that I didn't want to call Rona and refute it for fear that it might spin around and happen.

Several weeks later when I was in Palm Springs, a girl friend invited me to a party and Rona was there. We met and I liked her enormously. We talked for a long time, and I told her all kinds of things about our lives that she could have leaked, but she never did. She was very gracious to me and perhaps mildly amused at my childlike assessment of reality. She thought I was very naïve, and when she learned that I had serious theological and personal differences with Oral, she said to me, "You know they'll never let you stay, don't you?"

I said, "No, Rona, you're wrong. We are all Christians and we value marriage."

She said something to the effect of, "Honey, I know you think that, but I know how large corporations are run and you won't be there very long."

I laughed at her for her lack of spiritual insight and she laughed at me for my ignorance. But her words would turn out to be prophetic, and much sooner than I could have imagined.

CHAPTER TEN

Seed-Faith and Sanity

In 1977 I quit the weekly television show. For some time I had been getting increasingly dissatisfied with my job on the show. By this time I performed a solo or a duet on every program and occasionally did interviews with Oral. I had earned a solid position on the show, and there were many financial and professional benefits that went along with it. In a career sense it should have been enormously satisfying, but it wasn't.

I had discovered in the Bible that my heritage as a child of God was that I be peaceful and happy in my work. The job that God had assigned me to do should cause me peace and joy and satisfaction whether I liked the actual work or not. But I didn't have peace, and joy, and satisfaction over my work. I was ragged at the edges. The whole thing had become monotonous to me.

I couldn't get excited anymore about raising money for new buildings. Since I had started there in 1965 when there were only three little buildings, I had seen many of them go up. I was bored with watching the pattern repeat itself. We'd go to seminars, sing "The King Is Coming" or "He's Alive," share the goals of the university, and get people excited about the ministry. They'd respond by giving money and we'd use the money to build more buildings. I could rarely feel the movement of the Spirit in our shows or in our lives as I once had.

For a long time I had really loved the show, and in the first four or five years I would have died for it. It seemed to me as if we were on the cutting edge of something special then. But now, it was just a job. It paid well and I liked to sing, but I had come in with such high ideals, such great expectations, that reality just couldn't match it in the long run.

Now it seemed to me that all of our efforts revolved around fund-raising. We used sophisticated marketing techniques to sell Jesus, to make Him more attractive so more people would get involved and support what we were doing. I found that distasteful, and I commented on it at regular intervals. I had always thought the corporation existed to serve the ministry. Now it seemed the ministry was serving the corporation.

I still hadn't learned that prayer was the most effective form of protest, so I continually lobbed verbal grenades at Oral. When I felt he had preached too often on Seed-Faith I would say to Richard, "Don't you think it's time for Oral to preach on healing again?" or, "Richard, when was the last time Oral presented the plan of salvation?" Although my questions were always couched in innocence, I'm sure Oral and Richard both were aware of the edge they carried.

The Seed-Faith theology that Oral had developed bothered me a great deal because I saw that, when taken to its natural extremes, it reduced God to a sugar daddy. If you wanted His blessings and His love, you paid Him off. Over and over again we heard Oral say, "Give out of your need." I began to question the motivation that kind of giving implied. Were we giving to God out of our love and gratitude to Him or were we bartering with Him? I do believe in the laws of sowing and reaping, and I believe that when you give to God with a pure heart, you will receive blessings from Him in return. The Scripture is very clear that if you give generously, you will receive generously, "pressed down, shaken together and running over." But it is also very clear about what is to be the motive for our giving.

In Luke 6:32–37 Jesus admonishes His disciples *not* to give with the expectation of return. "And if you are kind and good and do favors to and benefit those who are kind and good and do favors to and benefit you, what quality of credit is that to you? For even the preeminently sinful do the same. And if you lend money at interest to those from whom you hope to receive, what quality of credit and thanks is that to you? Even notorious sinners lend money at interest to sinners so as to recover much gain. But love your enemies, and be kind and do good to them, and lend, expecting and hoping for *nothing* in return."

The distinction may appear to be too subtle and I know Oral thought I was splitting theological hairs, but it seemed supremely important to me. If we give to God because we think that by giving we have somehow placed Him in our debt and He is now required to come through for us and meet our needs, we have, I believe, perverted the heart of the Gospel. Our only motive for giving should be love. When we encouraged people to give in order to have their needs met or so that they would receive "a hundredfold in return," I believed we were appealing to their sense of greed or desperation, neither of which seemed admirable to me. It was a wonderful fund-raising tool, but I believe it gave people a very unbalanced view of a very important biblical principle.

At the time, I was taking a humanities course from the university and my professor was discussing Martin

Luther and the Reformation. When we started looking at the abuses in the Catholic Church that Luther had wanted to reform, I began to see parallels in our situation. Luther was incensed by the Church's practice of selling indulgences—offering forgiveness of sin and a shorter period of time in purgatory in return for gifts to the church. I had a very difficult time distinguishing between the selling of indulgences and the concept of Seed-Faith inflated to the degree to which we had inflated it. Of course, Oral was more subtle. He never promised salvation in exchange for gifts to his ministry, but there were still many people who believed that God was going to look at them in a kindlier way and perhaps their son would get off drugs or they would get their drunken husband into heaven if they gave money to Oral Roberts.

So I asked my professor, "What's the difference?" and one day I looked at him and said, "Where's our Martin Luther? We need one right now. Where is he?" But he was an intelligent man and he knew I was skating on thin ice so without comment he packed up his blackboard and left. I began to lose heart after that.

Several months later, as I was sitting in my bathtub one afternoon, I began looking around at the opulent appointments of the bathroom. The bathtub itself was seven feet long with a gold swan for a tap, and directly over it hung a gold and crystal chandelier. The room, which was as large as the master bedroom in many homes, was decorated with mirrors, marble, and yellow Chinese wallpaper. A thick yellow carpet covered the floor, and a chaise longue stood on the opposite side of the room. Often, after emerging from a bath, I would wrap myself in thirsty, thick yellow towels, recline on the lounge and talk to my friends on one of the three phones in the room. As I looked at all of this luxury, I thought to myself, "This should be making me happy—but it's not."

I picked up the phone by the bathtub and called Al Bush, who had been president of the Oral Roberts Evangelical Association for many years. As nearly as I can remember, the conversation went something like this:

"Al," I said, "in the forty shows that we taped last year, how many times did we give people the plan of salvation?"

"The plan of salvation? Gosh, Patti, I don't know. I'm sure we must have given it to them at least once," he said.

"And how many times did we give them the principles of Seed-Faith?"

He laughed. "Patti, you know the answer to that. We give the principles of Seed-Faith on every show. What's all this about?"

"Al, in the letters that you received from viewers, how many of them thought that maybe if they gave money to Oral, they had bought a little place in the Kingdom? How many may have thought that swayed God's opinion about their eternal destiny?"

He didn't answer for a long time. When he finally replied he lowered his voice and said soberly and a bit hesitantly, "A whole lot of them did, Patti."

I hung up and stared angrily at the gold swan. It suddenly represented all the incongruities of my life. It was glossy and beautiful and it performed its function well, but it had no heart, no life. Our lives seemed like that to me. On the surface everything looked beautiful and we performed like parts of a well-oiled machine, which we were. But in many ways we were as cold and as lifeless and as pretentious as the gold swan, which I now imagined was silently mocking me. I was suddenly filled with rage and if I could have grabbed its mouth and twisted it till it closed, I would have. I was so tired of the ambiguities of my life. I hated feeling that I and my opinions were tolerated simply because I was a serviceable part of the machine. "Curse you, swan," I hissed through clenched teeth. "I don't know if it's possible to live any more without feeling as if I have sold a piece of my soul, but if it is, I want to find out how to do it."

Although my rage and confusion were genuine, there was something a little disturbing about them. On one hand I was sickened by the excesses and the pretenses of my life. I felt Oral was being manipulative in his fund raising, but, on the other hand, I enjoyed its fruits. If I had indeed sold my soul, I had done so willingly. I could not now turn around and complain that the price had been too high. I couldn't have it both ways. That was something Oral and Richard understood much better than I did. I'm sure Richard in particular found my complaints a little hypocritical when he saw the bills I ran up every month. My extravagance blunted any prophetic impact I might have had.

That night, I talked to Richard about quitting the show. I said, "I don't want to work on the TV show anymore. I want to stay home for a while."

At first he was very insecure about the idea, but when he realized that I was serious, he told me that I would have to write a formal letter of resignation to Oral, who was officially my boss.

So I sent Oral a letter in which I told him that I had loved the show and appreciated everything he had done for me, but that I wanted to leave television for a while.

Shortly, I received a letter back from Ron Smith, Chief of Staff of the Oral Roberts Ministries, which said, "Dear Patti, we accept your resignation." Period. I never got any official response from Oral. Occasionally when Richard and I would visit Oral and Evelyn at home, he would tease me, "Hey, Patrick (his pet nickname for me), whatcha gonna do now that you're not working for us?" and I'd say, "Oh, Oral, I'm just going to stay home." Which I did, for a long time.

The ORU students began to ask questions about my absence, but the school never made any direct inquiry into why I quit. Evelyn was appointed to explain my absence. She squelched the rumors that I was pregnant or that Richard and I were getting a divorce. She told people that my children were at an age when they needed my attention and that I was going to stay home and take care of them.

Some members of the TV audience also asked where I was, but there was never any announcement made when I left the show and never any official explanation given. It was as if I had just disappeared or had never been on the show at all.

A few months after I quit, I began casting about for something to do. I still felt that God had something special for me to do with my life, and I began to try to discover what it was. I began to look for the "mission field," wherever that might be, because that was the original "vision" Oral had imparted to me as a student at ORU. He had taught us to "go into all the world" with the message, and I began to wonder, "Can I do that? Maybe my calling is just to be Richard's and Oral's eyes and ears on the mission field."

I explained that to Richard, and he said, "I'm sure that's it." He wrote a fund-raising letter with me, saying, "My wife is going to places where I cannot go, and it's like having two of me. I am at home with my calling here, and she is overseas acting as my foreign eyes. We are working together to accomplish God's plan."

I set up an office in the fourth bedroom of our house and hired Beverly Hubbard, my old college friend who had just returned from Poland, as my secretary. At this time Richard and I were both receiving many invitations to sing in churches around the country. Since I was now free from my obligations to the television show, I began to accept more of these offers. The money I received I used for my overseas outreach. I really had no thought of starting my own organization, but Richard decided he didn't want that income on our joint tax return, so I incorporated as PRIO.

My first overseas trip was to England. I felt very strongly that England was prepared for revival and that God was going to do wonderful things, so I did a singing tour there. I made two trips to England. The results each time were gratifying, but the major revival that I had anticipated did not materialize at that time.

I also felt a great warmth in my heart for Iran and the countries of the Middle East. Several years earlier, on a trip to London with Richard, I had met a young Iranian student, Masood Molavi. He had become good friends with our family and under his influence I had developed a great concern for the Muslim world and particularly Iran.

My first trip to Iran originated accidentally. I had gone to Taiwan on a one-week missionary trip, and when it was over I decided to come home by way of Iran. It was a spur-of-the-moment decision, prompted by my intense curiosity over the country. I called Masood in London, and he said he would arrange to have his parents pick me up at the Tehran airport. I didn't have a visa, but I had read in a travel brochure that sometimes you could get in without one, so I decided to try. I booked a reservation on Pan Am's around-the-world flight and arrived in Tehran at 2:00 A.M., alone, knowing no one, without a visa, and not speaking the language.

At first, airport officials refused to let me in the country. But after two hours of heated discussion and a host of flash prayers on my part, they finally issued me a temporary visa.

I rounded up my suitcases and began looking for someone who might be looking for me. I had no idea what the Molavis looked like but I spotted a man holding a cardboard sign with two words written in what I supposed to be English. The first word started with P and the second with R. Other than that it bore no resemblance to my name. I walked up to him and rather timidly introduced myself. In broken English he welcomed me and pantomimed the message that the family was delighted to have me as a guest.

I spent a week with the Molavis and absolutely fell in love with the family and with Iran. After that I made three more trips to the Middle East. I spent a total of eight weeks there over a period of two years. On my third trip, I took a group of ten singers and musicians from ORU. That trip cost $22,000. I borrowed $15,000 from a Tulsa bank and Richard gave me $7,000. He later joined us in Iran, where we received a warm welcome. Our little group sang for churches, prayer groups, U.S. military personnel, at a Muslim women's college and on Iranian national TV. To my knowledge, that was the first and only time a Christian group ever appeared on television in Iran.

My overseas travels were like a breath of fresh air. Since Iran is predominantly Muslim, it had none of the focus of the Christian culture that I found so stifling in America. No one really even knew who I was. I was free from the Roberts image and was able to be just a simple believer fellowshiping with other believers.

The only dark spot in my travels was having to leave my children. Of course, they were used to both Richard and me being gone when we had to tape television shows on location, but I still missed them terribly and felt enormous guilt about leaving them. There were times when I could hardly bear to hear their voices on the telephone, but life had become so miserable within the Roberts compound that the agony of staying became worse than the agony of going. The ministry provided a legitimate excuse for me to run, and I took it. I would lie in bed at night and see in my imagination the word *Iran* split into two words, *I-ran*. My guilt over my children was eased somewhat by the knowledge that I was leaving them in very capable hands. We had a live-in housekeeper and nanny, a middle-aged woman named Idella. A staunch Baptist, Idella sort of mothered all of us. I cried on her shoulder many times, and I know Richard often confided in her also. She literally kept our house and our lives running.

With my departure from the show, almost all communication between Richard and me had ceased. I was treated more and more as an outsider, someone who could not be trusted. In a way, I think both Richard and Oral were relieved by my decision—Richard because our domestic tension was eased when I was out of the country, and Oral, because I increasingly questioned his operations.

Shortly after I quit the show, Oral had announced his intention to build the City of Faith and I had not felt a part of that vision. I believed in joining the healing streams of medicine and faith together but I didn't think we needed a $500 million complex in a city that already had too many hospital beds, to accomplish that. I thought Oral should have remained true to his original concept of touching people on the mission field—whether that was in India, where people were dying for lack of the most basic medical care, or New York City, where the light of faith had grown dim.

I never argued with Oral about the hospital but he knew I did not support him and as long as I was an active member of his ministry, available to the press, I was somewhat of a threat. It would have been devastating, especially in the early days of the City of Faith controversy, for any member of the family to have been quoted in the *Tulsa Tribune* agreeing with Oral's opponents. Better to have dissenters safely out of the way, ministering to the Muslims in Iran.

There was nothing cruel about this on Oral's part. I do not think that even then he actively disliked me. But Oral was always a total realist. There is a well-known story in circulation about an imagined conversation between himself and the ORU basketball coach that illustrates his total practicality.

The coach comes to Oral one day and says, "President Roberts, our basketball team has won all of its games this season. What do you think of that?" "I think that's wonderful," Oral says. "You are doing a terrific job as a coach and we all love you." After thinking a moment, the coach asks him, "What if we don't win as many of our games next season? Will you still love me?" Oral replies immediately, "We'll love you, but we'll miss you."

Oral knew a year before Richard and I finally admitted it to ourselves that our marriage was over. With my insistence (crippled as it was by my own inconsistencies) that marriage was more important than ministry, and my views on Seed-Faith, I was not a suitable wife for Richard. Oral tried very hard one night to convince me to stop prolonging the agony.

Richard and I had gone to Oral and Evelyn's after dinner. We were both under great stress and we wanted to talk to them. Evelyn and Richard went into Evelyn's bedroom, and Oral and I stayed in the den.

We made polite small talk for a few minutes. Then Oral said to me, "Patti, why don't the two of you just get a divorce? I'll just tell my partners you couldn't make it, and we'll let the chips fall where they may. I don't see any point in cutting the tail off the dog in small pieces. Why don't you lop it off and that will be that? Richard is not happy in his work, he's not performing well, he's not functioning well. Just get it over and go on from there."

I knew in my heart that he was right, but I just wasn't ready to admit defeat yet. I said, "Oral, I can't. I just can't do it. I've got to try. We've both got to try."

He said, "Well, I don't see the point," and we ended the discussion.

I don't know what Evelyn said to Richard, and I never told him of my conversation with Oral. We walked home in silence, but inside we were both crying out, "What next, God? Where do we go from here?"

Several months later I had a very strange dream. At the time it both horrified and frightened me, but since then I have often wondered if it was perhaps God's answer to my "what next" question. I still do not understand everything that it included, but in many ways it did foreshadow the tragic events that were soon to come.

I had gone out to Palm Springs to open up our house there and Richard was going to join me as soon as he could get away. It was one night not long after I had arrived that I had this dream.

I was looking for Richard and I knew that he was in the

big warehouse building. The building was tall and square, of brown wooden clapboard construction, and there was an outside entrance to the second floor which contained a meat packing plant. They only dealt in lamb and they would cut it up, package it, and send it out. The bottom floor was a large empty room, dark and dusty from disuse. The ceiling was very high except that, to the right as you entered, there was an alcove that had a dropped ceiling. In the alcove was a bar where you could get popcorn and cokes.

Richard and about six of the World Action Singers were sitting there, laughing and joking. They were very loud, screaming with laughter. I went over and spoke to Richard and he looked at me as if to say, "What are you doing here?" He wasn't happy to see me. There was an edge in the air and conflict between us, although I couldn't pinpoint the cause of it. My very presence seemed to annoy him. It was as if I were a serious ogre and I was throwing a wet blanket on their hilarity.

There were a few people milling about in this warehouse as if they were in an art gallery, but there were no pictures on the wall. They were all staring at something, but I didn't know what.

Over in the back right corner on a small square platform was a diamond cutter. He was concentrating his whole mental and spiritual capacities on making the right cut. I went over to him and I started weeping because it was so noisy in there and nobody was helping him and he was trying so hard. Somehow I knew that he wasn't a Christian, and he looked as if that diamond was his whole life. Everyone was making it so difficult for him with all that noise and inattentiveness. They didn't care about him, and I became so angry I said to Richard, "Why don't you help him?" He said, "Patti, go away." I was terribly distraught, but everyone else thought I was stupid for being so upset. Their attitude was, "You dummy, he's just cutting a diamond."

I went over to watch and on the way a lady accosted me and began berating me. "Why aren't you on the show any more?" she questioned. "Don't you know God put you there? How dare you have Richard to stand there and preach the Gospel without you by his side?" She went on and on yelling at me right in front of this diamond cutter. I finally grabbed her by the shoulders and said, "Stop it, stop it! You're going to make him break it." She quit shouting at me, but the noise in the room was still deafening.

My attention was distracted then by the sound of a bell. I suddenly noticed that there were four square holes in the ceiling from which they discarded things from the meat packing center. When the bell rang, everyone stopped talking and rushed over to this net that was hanging on the far left side of the wall. There was a layer of heavy netting, the kind that oranges are often bagged in, and on top of that was a thick layer of pressed flesh and then another layer of netting. The people stretched this on the floor under the four holes. Bits of bone with lamb on them and fat and debris from the meat packing plant would drop through and they would catch it. That's what they were there for, to catch the bones and fat.

I thought that was the strangest thing. They could go right upstairs and get all the lamb they wanted instead of scrambling for the leftovers. But they either didn't know that or they didn't want to do it. What they couldn't eat they collected in little bags and then went back to their tables and began telling jokes again.

The room got very loud again and the lady resumed

her tirade. I was standing by the diamond cutter saying, "He's going to break it; he's going to break it," and he broke it. Again I cried, but he just kept on cutting as if he didn't know anything had happened, while the diamond lay shattered in a hundred glistening pieces on the cutting table. He was trying so hard.

I ran over to Richard and said, "Don't you see what all of you have made him do? Your laughter was so loud that he couldn't concentrate. Richard, he broke it. He broke the diamond!" I started swearing and he swore back at me. I ran out of the room and he ran after me, swearing.

That was the end of the dream.

I woke up and began to sob because I knew I had seen what appeared to be the end. Wave after wave of futility and hopelessness washed over me. I realized I would never change anything. No matter what *I* said or did, they would still be there eating the fat and bones. The diamond cutter would be there trying but nothing I could say would make any difference. I sat up in my bed and screamed.

"Please, God, no! No, oh please, no," I cried. *Instead of having the lamb of God*, I thought, *Richard and those he works with are content with this trash. They are celebrating leftovers. God help us up to the second floor.*

It was the mystery of their being thrilled with the bits of meat left on a discarded bone, when all they had to do was go upstairs to get all the lamb they wanted, the hurt of seeing them enjoy that bone, that got to me. It was the frustration of that woman not understanding why I left the show, the sorrow of that man and the sense that whatever I had seen appeared immutable, that crushed me. I believed it was a panoramic view of the end, and it terrified me. I pulled the covers up around me and huddled in my bed like a frightened animal. I was afraid to sleep, afraid of what I might dream if I closed my eyes again. I sat immobilized, while my heart beat so hard and so fast it made the bed jiggle. It wasn't until the sun finally came up and I could hear the day beginning that I relaxed. Comforted by the noise of birds whistling to each other and the chg-chg-chg of the automatic sprinkler system watering the back yard, I fell into a restless sleep.

CHAPTER ELEVEN

End of Charade

December 5, 1978, is a day that will remain forever etched in my memory.

I was standing in the kitchen, pouring myself a cup of hot tea, when I heard Richard's key opening the back door. I glanced quickly at the clock hanging over the sink. It was 9:00 P.M. "He's home early," I thought.

Richard had gone to Florida on a fishing trip with Oral and Evelyn. I had stayed home because the tensions in our marriage were so unbearable that Richard and I needed the time away from each other and from the family. We were all unhappy, and when we were together, our misery seemed compounded. We never expressed our displeasure any more. The time for honest communication had long since passed. Now we responded to each other with calculated civility. We spoke from hearts of stainless steel, and each word was pure, concentrated hostility. We had honed our politeness to a razor's edge, and now it was smooth and cold and hard. Hatred would have been a step up for us. At least with hatred we might have experienced some fire, some passion, some human emotion. We were sitting on a warhead and we both knew it. When it would explode or where, or what would happen when it did were questions too horrible and too frightening to contemplate, so we continued to walk gingerly through our lives, breathing a prayer of relief each night that we had made it through one more day.

Richard was breezing through the house now, whistling. It was the most cheerful sound I'd heard from him in months. "The trip must have done him good," I thought.

"Patti," he called. "I've got some great news. Come into the bedroom where we can talk."

My curiosity aroused, I followed Richard into the room and shut the door behind me. Something in the tone of his voice made me uneasy. I didn't know what had happened in Florida, but my stomach started to knot and I began to feel chilled.

I sat down in one of the little English chintz-covered chairs by the sofa and cast him an inquiring glance, which he answered with an enigmatic smile. He seemed keyed up and excited—nervous.

Watching him pace up and down before the sliding glass doors, still in his fishing clothes, I was struck by how charming Rich could be. When he was excited he had a little boy quality that was very endearing. I hadn't noticed it in a long time. It, too, had gotten lost in all the years of hostility.

Finally he settled on the sofa and, taking my hand in his, said, "Patti, this charade has gone on long enough. I've talked to Mother and Dad and they've given me permission to get a divorce and I want one right away. There's just no point in this marriage any longer.

"Now, I don't want you to worry because I'm going to take care of you. In the next few days we'll get together with the lawyers and we'll work it out. But," he added, "I don't have long to work on it because on January 2 we start taping, so it's got to be settled by then because I want to go to California. So I want you to find a house in the next few days and I'll give you the down payment. Go ahead and get your stuff moved out. We'll work it out together with the children."

For a moment everything in the room seemed to stop. I could feel my heart pounding, and my hands were clammy. I opened my mouth to speak but couldn't find words.

Mercifully, the doorbell rang then and Richard went to answer it. I sat still, unable to move. My mind raced in a thousand directions. I was stunned, not so much by Richard's request for a divorce—I had contemplated divorce and had planned to ask him for one after Christmas—but by his casual, almost exuberant attitude about it. It was as if he were reporting on a board meeting that had gone well. A difficult problem had been solved and he was relieved to have found an answer. Our marriage problems weren't such a heart-wrenching dilemma after all. They could be dealt with on a fishing trip, without even consulting one of the principals.

My thoughts were interrupted by the sound of voices and laughter coming from the hall. Our visitor was Beverly. Richard brought her into the bedroom and she sat on a chair opposite me, glancing curiously in my direction, while Richard resettled himself on the sofa. I still had not spoken, but now I found my voice and greeted her.

Richard, seeming not to notice the effect his announcement had on me, turned to Beverly and said, "Guess what, Beverly?"

"What?"

"We're getting a divorce," . . . and with just a comma, not a period, he added, "and I couldn't be happier."

Beverly's eyes flew right to me. I smiled wanly and shrugged, as Richard continued. As if to shelter himself from the disorientation and hurt I knew he must also be feeling, he embarked on a well-rehearsed speech.

"You know, this marriage has never worked, and I don't see any point in dragging it on and on. I'm going to go on in the ministry and she's going to go on and do her own thing and it's going to work out great. Beverly, I know you love us both and I don't want you to worry about either of us."

Then he sat back, crossed his legs on the coffee table and said, "Oh, Beverly, you've got to help me. In my work I need to be married, so I know I'll remarry within a year. But the problem is going to be that women are absolutely going to come out of the woodwork when they find out I'm single. What am I going to do?"

At that point, I lost touch with the rest of the conversation. My own thoughts drowned out what Richard and Beverly were saying, and I didn't hear anything else the rest of the evening. I wasn't even aware of Beverly's leaving. The next thing I remember was getting to my feet about midnight and saying to Richard, "Well, I guess we shouldn't sleep together any more, so I'll go sleep with the children." Although it would be several months before we would be legally divorced, I felt divorced from that moment on. To have slept with Richard that night would have been like crawling into bed with a stranger and pretending to be married.

I grabbed a pillow from our bed and stumbled down the hall to the children's room. Cracking open the door, I slipped in quietly so as not to wake them, and fell across the spare bed. I slept with my clothes on, too tired and too numb to even undress or to think about what was going to happen to us all now.

The next day the children knew something was wrong, so Richard and I called them together in Juli's bedroom. He held Christi on his lap and I cradled Juli in my arms. Richard told them, "Mommy and Daddy are getting a divorce. We're not happy with each other and we don't love each other any more. You're going to live with Mommy, but I'll always be your Daddy and you can come visit me." We both assured them that it was not their fault we were divorcing.

Juli immediately burst into tears. "Well, this means we can't go to Palm Springs for Christmas, doesn't it?" she asked. At six she couldn't comprehend the finality of divorce, and she reacted with typical childlike honesty. Christmas at Palm Springs had become a family tradition, and some of our happiest times had been spent there. We would all miss it.

Christi let out a big sigh and said, "Mommy, I thought you were dying of some disease or something. We knew something was wrong because you went to bed right after dinner every night. You mean you're not going to die? You're not even sick?"

"No, I'm not sick," I said.

"Boy, is that a relief. Whew."

They were both stunned, but their childish reactions to the news in many ways mirrored our own attitudes. At this point, we had given very little thought to the long-range and very public consequences of our decision. We very naïvely assumed that we could arrange a friendly, quiet divorce. The error of that assumption would soon be viciously exposed. Our divorce would be neither friendly nor private.

CHAPTER TWELVE

Shock Waves

Now that we had decided to get a divorce, Richard and I both wanted to expedite things as much as possible. I began looking for a place to live and finally settled on a condominium next door to my brother Ron. We had agreed that Richard would keep the Tulsa residence and I would keep the furniture from the Palm Springs house, so on December 16 I flew out to California to collect it.

Before I left, Richard mentioned that Evelyn had expressed concern that since we were divorcing she would no longer be able to see the children. He asked me to stop by and reassure her while I was in California.

She and Oral had a home in Palm Springs about two blocks up the hill from ours, so while the moving men were packing up my furniture, I picked up a few things that they had loaned us and drove up to their house.

I rang the bell and Evelyn answered the door. It was a very awkward, hurtful moment, but Evelyn displayed no anger or desire for recrimination toward me. No one had gotten to the point yet of needing to assign blame. It was still our private family pain. The world didn't know about it yet so there wasn't any need to blame anybody.

Evelyn and I talked for a few minutes and I said, "I've just come to tell you that even though Richard and I are divorcing, the children aren't divorcing anybody and I want you not to forget them. Love them and take time with them and just know that you have perfect freedom to spend time with them. They're going to need that. There's no reason they should be punished for what's happening in our lives."

That was a very naïve statement because children ultimately bear the greatest punishment in a divorce. Maybe that's why they always think they caused it. Since they're the ones who suffer the most, they feel they must be to blame.

While Evelyn and I were talking, I could hear hammering going on in the back of the house. Then Oral yelled, "Patrick, come here." I walked into his office and saw that he and his two jet pilots were hanging pictures. Oral asked me, "Do you think that picture's high enough? Does it look good on that wall?"

I looked at him in amazement and said, "Yeah, Oral, it looks wonderful." Our whole lives were falling apart and he wanted to know about pictures. He didn't have anything to say about the divorce. He just said, "Well, Patrick, we'll see ya, honey." Evelyn and I burst into tears, and we hugged each other and said goodbye. That was the last time I had any truly personal contact with them.

People used to say to me, "Surely Oral and Evelyn fought this divorce; surely they counseled you." I just laughed. I think there comes a time when pain is so intense or the sense of futility so heavy, even for great spiritual leaders, and it is so close to you that you don't counsel, you don't do anything, you let it happen. And we all let it happen. By this time we were all weakened by the years and years of pain. And the City of Faith battles were so intense at this same time that Oral was fighting for the life of his dream every day. My marriage was just one more battle, and he simply didn't have the time or the strength to fight it too. He had reached his limit.

I flew home and on December 18 the men from the university maintenance crew arrived with moving trucks. Richard had arranged for them to move the rest of my things into the condo from what had suddenly become his house alone. From this point on, I was not allowed to return.

Once settled in my new home, I turned my attention to Christmas. I had to do shopping, decorate the house, and try to provide as normal a holiday for the children as I could. My mother flew down from Oregon and she did most of the decorating and the Christmas baking. Much of the time I was simply too numb to function very effectively. Everything frightened me and nothing frightened me. I was fearless and wracked with fears. It was like walking through a minefield. You're terrified, but the only way to get through is to walk fearlessly to the other side, even though you feel you are totally paralyzed.

Beverly would come over after work and find me just sitting, staring out the window, and she would shake me and say, "Look, we're going to make it through this. God is going to help. They can't eat you up and swallow you."

At that time Richard and I both had signs on our desks that read, "The battle is the Lord's." It was as if we thought that somehow God was going to choose sides in this conflict between two of His children. We were trying to use God as shields against each other. God did have shields for us, but it was against our problems and the ignorant way in which we had tried to build our lives.

I spent most of my days at the lawyer's office. We were prepared to go to court if necessary, and building our case involved a continuous cycle of gathering evidence, taking depositions, and other matters. It took three months of daily work to complete the paperwork.

As word of the divorce leaked out, the Robertses were forced into a defensive posture. It seemed that every time I turned around, Richard was on some national TV broadcast saying how hurt he was that I had deserted him. The ORU paper ran several stories that said the same thing, and Oral was repeating it to some of his partners. Each time I heard it it would throw me into a rage. They had broken the no-fault pact we had agreed upon. I wanted to call the newspapers and defend myself. But fortunately, Ron and my lawyer convinced me that I had nothing to gain by that.

I was really a little surprised that things had taken this bad a turn because when Richard asked me for a divorce, he had told me, "Look, I don't hate you, and you don't hate me. It's just not working out and we're not going to do this any more. It's not going to be a big deal. It will be a quiet divorce." And I think he meant it. But once the news began to leak out, the publicity began to affect the mail, and when the mail is affected, the money slows. They had committed themselves to a huge budget to finance the hospital, and they couldn't chance the money's being affected. The machine began nipping at their heels and they had to pacify it. I think under less pressured circumstances the divorce would have been handled with much more civility. I don't think they would have reacted the way they did if they hadn't had so much to protect.

In my more lucid moments I realized that had I been in their shoes I would probably have reacted the same way and that knowledge angered me more than anything. To see how institutions, even Christian ones, could destroy people, could cause good people to do very bad things, enraged me. I felt that the "machine" had destroyed Oral's family, it had destroyed mine, and it still would not be pacified. It was a lion that must continually be fed, and we were all being sacrificed to it.

The shock had continual waves. Students at ORU were hurt and confused. Two people whom they had loved were getting a divorce and no one was providing an adequate explanation. The media were also pressing for information. Confronted with this pressure, Oral, Richard, and Evelyn had to find a scapegoat for the sake of corporate expediency. They had no choice but to fault me. But I knew that at one time they had loved me. I don't believe they were so heartless that they derived pleasure from seeing the girls and me injured by receiving the short end of the publicity stick. They didn't have any other choice. Outside of rethinking their entire theology and professional goals, there was no other option available to them.

The crowning blow came one day in January. I was standing in my kitchen talking to my mother and Ron, who was still working for Richard. The phone rang and it was Richard. He asked to speak to Ron, and when Ron answered he said, "I have a letter for Patti and I want you to come and get it."

Ron went over and picked it up and brought it back to me. I sensed even before I opened it that it was going to be bad news, but I had no idea how bad. The letter, which presented itself as a reconciliation letter, stated that Richard loved me and wanted to try again to make our marriage work. It accused me of being an unfit wife to Richard and of leaving him to start my own ministry. It quoted Ephesians 5:22,23 and asked that I return home, submit myself to Richard as the Scriptures commanded, and resume my responsibilities as his wife and the mother of our children. It specified that I must give up singing, even with Richard, give up PRIO, fire my secretary, our nanny and the housekeeper, and stay at home.

I was devastated. I couldn't believe that the letter represented an honest attempt at reconciliation. It seemed to me that someone must have decided that a reconciliation attempt had to be made and so a letter was composed that could be used as a publicity instrument if need be.

I wept until I thought my insides were going to fall out. I sobbed until my face swelled and my stomach hurt. I thought I was going to die. There was something so vicious about the letter that it seemed to me the ultimate cruelty.

It took me several days to compose myself and, with the help of my lawyer, to draft a response. I pointed out that Richard had always said that I was a good wife and that he had supported me in my ministry. I reminded him of his responsibilities to be the spiritual head of our family and I told him I would come home, I would give up my ministry, I would reconcile. I'd close my office, and fire my nanny, but I also requested that if I made that sacrifice, that he would leave his father's ministry temporarily and seek professional counseling with me.

His response was negative. He would not reconcile under those conditions. The attempt at reconciliation had been political on both sides. There was no ounce of real love between us. Neither of us had a heart for reconciliation. We both just wanted to save face with the public. So, he called my hand and I called his. Both were empty.

After the reconciliation fiasco, things moved quickly to

a climax. By March 8 we had worked out the remaining legal problems and I had filed for divorce.

The night before the divorce was finalized, Richard called me. There was a gentle concern in his voice that I hadn't heard in months. It was our last caring encounter. He said, "Patti, you know tomorrow the newspapers are going to be after you for a story. Be careful what you say. Know that from now on, there will be those who will try to hurt you. You don't know whom you can trust any more." I was stunned. I didn't know what to say to him. I felt as if it was just his last effort to touch me. I guess the last thing he could do was to say, "I can't help you now. A good many churches will turn against you. It may be over for your career. I'm sorry it's that way, but that's just the nature of life. You know," he said with an uncertain little laugh, "we've both heard it said that the Christian army is the only one that shoots its wounded. Well, we're both wounded right now. I have Mother and Father and the ministry to offer me some protection, but you don't have any protection now, so be careful." And with that, he hung up.

Richard's call was strangely tender. I knew that he was genuinely hurting that night. The tragedy was that we could never hurt together.

CHAPTER THIRTEEN

Captured by Fear

Immediately after the divorce, my life went into a spiral of confusion, hurt and tremendous rage. I had an extreme need to be affirmed as a person and as a woman. The divorce had left me feeling so extraneous to the human race that I needed constant reassurance that I was pretty, that I was feminine, that I could sing. I wasn't sure of any of these things any more.

I felt that I had not mattered as a wife or as a mother or even as a member of the ministry, and I sought continuously to find some place where I could matter. I poured a lot of my grief and anger into the recording of an album. It contained ten songs, all written by me and all having little meaning but to express sorrow. To this day, it lies under the bed in the guest room.

I made many bad decisions during those first few months—bad business choices as well as personal choices. My mother and Beverly thought I was going to have a nervous breakdown. When I talked, I repeated myself a lot and even began to stutter. I was very confused and I became very paranoid. Things that ordinarily were easy became difficult for me. Going to the grocery store was tough. I felt that everyone was staring at me. Therefore, I hibernated a lot, just staying inside my condominium. My biggest pastime became gourmet cooking. I entertained a lot at home but seldom went out. I just didn't have the strength to go outside the house, because outside was Tulsa, and in the section where I lived, everything reminded me of the life I no longer had. Every time I passed ORU it seemed to me that even the buildings cried out to mock me, "We won, we won. You're a nonperson. You don't matter."

It was difficult for me to gauge exactly how the public was reacting to the news of our divorce, because after I moved into the condo, I received very little of the mail that was sent to me at the association or at Richard's house. The reaction at ORU was volatile with many un-answered questions. The students and the faculty were outraged, and on two different occasions, forums were held on campus to try to explain what had happened. I did not attend either one. I had been told that I would not be allowed on campus and that if I attempted to attend, the university guard would probably remove me. I never put them to the test so I don't know whether that was true or not.

My girls were suffering from the traumas that only the children of the famous encounter. The newspapers were full of news about the divorce and about the City of Faith controversy. I was experiencing my own pain, but they were seeing their mother, their father, their grand-parents—everyone they loved—being held up to public comment. Many of the children who attended their school were children of ORU professors. They experi-enced one cut after another on their hearts. We seemed to be knee-deep in blood most of the time.

One night I put them to bed and went downstairs to play the piano. I was so depressed I began to cry: "God, there's nothing in the world but insanity, there's nothing in our lives but madness and some of it is coming from the religious establishment. All of us, everyone whose last name is Roberts, is being accused and criticized at every turn. Religion is a costly thing to be involved in right now. God, how do I tell my children that Your name is not religion? That you are Love?" As I sat there silently talking to God, a song began to form in my mind. It was a lullaby, and I believe He gave the first verse to my children and the second to me.

> My peace I give to you
> It's a peace the world cannot know.
> Clouds of peace surround you
> Wherever your feet may go
> Protected by my angels
> And covered in my grace
> I'll never, never leave you
> We will win this long, long race
>
> When fear captures you in its dark embrace
> And your heart freezes in its place
> When the last drop of courage drains out of the cup
> And your strength can't last through the race
> When sorrow's knife has laid you bare
> And your soul is wounded by the pain
> Fear not, my child, you are not alone
> I'm here and I comfort my own.*

Many people have asked me why, if things were so uncomfortable, I remained in Tulsa so long after the divorce. I stayed because I didn't have the strength to go. I knew that my chances for living a whole and meaningful life in Tulsa were slim. In Tulsa I would always be defined by my past, but I was still confused regarding the present, and until some sensibility took over again, some

---

capacity to think and respond clearly, I just couldn't do anything to find a future.

Also, somewhere in the back of my mind I thought that maybe I should stay in Tulsa until I was certain that there was no possibility of reconciliation for Richard and me. I thought that, after the dust settled, perhaps we would see each other differently.

And some surprisingly sweet things happened in Tulsa. I continued to attend First Methodist Church, and they loved me with a love that was not diminished by the failure of my marriage. Dr. Thomas, the senior minister, was a true pastor to me. He was very supportive, which I'm sure must have caused him difficulties at times because much of his congregation was made up of ORU students and faculty, but no one in that church ever rebuffed me. They accepted me with open arms while never once condemning Richard either. In fact, after the divorce, the church missions board voted to give me a monthly offering for my ministry. That took a lot of courage because many members of that board had been or were involved with Oral Roberts. They will never know how much that meant to me. It was a startling act of love, the more so because at the time my ministry had pretty much ground to a halt.

One other church, First Baptist of Tulsa, also opened its arms and its heart to me. I was shocked because First Baptist had never seemed particularly warm to those of us who held charismatic beliefs and they thought so unfavorably of divorced persons ministering in any way— or so I thought. But they invited me to sing. That, to me, expressed the very heart of God. When the chips are down, religion means nothing, doctrine means nothing. Doctrine cannot warm or heal you. Jesus, exemplified through the hands and hearts of His Church, heals you.

Dr. Warren Hultgren of First Baptist and Dr. L. D. Thomas of First Methodist laid down their doctrines and took up the heart of Jesus.

Reaction from other places was mixed. Stones were not thrown at me as I had been afraid they might, but my concert schedule decreased. It was a dramatic change from the days when I had been much in demand for my name and my celebrity status. I felt now that my only value was in my name, in my past. When I was no longer famous, I even questioned my value.

The churches reacted toward me in five basic ways. Some cancelled my concerts because they did not want a newly divorced person ministering. They felt I still had too much "blood on my hands." They knew I had too much anger, and hurt and bitterness to minister effectively.

Others refused to have me because they sincerely do not believe that divorced persons should ever be allowed to minister.

Some automatically sided with Oral. Their reactions seemed at the time purely political. They never attempted to ascertain the facts of the situation or even to cloak their refusal in spiritual terms.

A few took a more thoughtful position. They said to me, "Patti, this has happened in your life and God does demand purity. We're not throwing any stones, but we are going to watch you and just see who you are, what your life is like, and if that fragrance of the Holy Spirit comes through even in the midst of this destruction. Then we want you to come and minister. You need time—time for God to work in your life, time to heal— and we need time to assess what's happened, what this divorce actually means in the Church.

Some churches had me come and sing especially for

the purpose of ministering to me. After I got there, they would tell me, "We felt we should have you come because perhaps you need someone to minister to you." Some ministered to me financially; some were emotional healers. Some pastors took a fatherly interest in me, and some acted as priests.

For my part, I was resentful and angry toward everyone who refused to have me. My ego was so battered that I was desperate to find a Band-aid. I was frightened that I would never work again, that maybe I no longer had a future in Christian music. I couldn't find me any more I was just floating, and floating terrified me. I wanted desperately to fit somewhere, with something or somebody and feel somehow needed again.

Out of my desperation, I tried to use my "ministry" to validate myself. I was so afraid of becoming a nonperson that I would have used anything or anyone, including God, to restore my shattered self-concept. But the harder I tried, the less successful I was. God had placed me squarely in the middle of that battle which every human being has to fight—whether we will choose God's will (i.e., timing, verdicts) or our own ego needs. Until that issue was settled, all my efforts at building a new career were futile.

I felt so helpless and enraged, especially when I looked at others who were on the battlefield with me and who seemed to be able to manipulate God better than I could. In my frustration I wrote a song blistering them.

> Oh, it's easy to be spiritual, to do for God good
>   deeds,
> To call yourself to do His work
> Just to satisfy your needs.
> But spiritual ambition is Satan's clever tool,

Seducing and deceiving while he plays you for the
 fool.
Oh, I've seen men spend precious lives building
 uncommissioned dreams.
Then God withdraws His blessing and they are left
 with frantic schemes.
Then success becomes the master, a lion that must
 be fed,
And obedience to the voice of God, obedience lies
 dead.
But I don't want to dream my dreams and say that
 they're divine;
I want the voice that's calling me to be Your voice,
 not mine.
Oh, God, save me. Oh, God, save me. Oh, God
 save me; from false spirituality.
Oh, God, save me. Oh, God, save me. Oh, God
 save me; guard obedience in me.
Save me.*

It was my own spiritual ambition which disgusted me
the most, however. I was sickened by it and yet I couldn't
let it go. I clung to my own "frantic schemes" as a drowning man clings to anything that will help him stay afloat. I
whimpered around for a long time, and I fought with
God. I knew He had placed me in a darkroom in order to
develop my life, but I was afraid of the dark. I kicked and
screamed and pulled at the door handle until I finally
collapsed in a sobbing heap on the floor, too exhausted to
fight any longer.

When I finally stopped screaming, I began to hear the
sweet, tender voice of the Lord. Now, instead of its being
a prison, the darkroom became a womb. I knew that I
would not remain there forever. God's timer was run-

ning and it was only a matter of time before I would be released. But for the present I was content to enjoy the comfort and the security of that place. I felt loved, and secure and extravagantly cared for. The long, agonizing struggle was over, and I knew that God was doing something new and wonderful in my life.

I was so grateful that He had loved me too much to allow me to create a counterfeit, to settle for building my own empirical security blanket instead of the Kingdom of God. I wanted whatever God was bringing to birth in me to be born on His timetable. I had no desire to emerge from the womb a minute early.

CHAPTER FOURTEEN

A Place for
—Mending—

In January 1980, ten months after the divorce, Richard remarried. Now that reconciliation was no longer an issue, I suddenly felt that I had the freedom to move out of Tulsa and that God would guide the girls and me toward a new town or city, a new house, and a new life.

For several months I had been thinking about where I could move, when and if I had the freedom to do so. I knew that if I left Tulsa I wanted to move somewhere that I could improve my abilities as a songwriter and get into an environment in which I could learn about the music business. I didn't want to live in New York or Los Angeles, however, so the Nashville area was my remaining option.

Several years earlier, Richard and I had been in Nashville recording an album for the Paragon Label. One afternoon during a break, Joe Moscheo, a Paragon executive, and I had driven over to a little town named Franklin to go antiquing. All I could remember about the place was that it was located eighteen miles south of Nashville and looked like a movie set for a confederate war drama. It was raining that day, but I was totally charmed by the town. Now I began to think about it again. The only side of Nashville I had seen was the studio side, and it did not seem to me to be a suitable place to raise two children. Franklin, on the other hand, had a wholesome atmosphere about it. It seemed to be the kind of town where people cut the grass instead of smoking it. To me it was the personification of Small Town, U.S.A., and instinctively I felt it would be a good place to raise a family.

One weekend shortly after Richard's marriage, I was in Atlanta doing a concert and decided on the spur of the moment to fly over to Nashville and visit Franklin again. I wanted to see if it was really as charming as I had remembered. I also decided that while I was there I would see what sort of housing was available, so I called Joe Moscheo and asked him if he could recommend a realtor to me. The next day I flew to Nashville, took a taxi to Franklin and met with the realtor. When I told him I was interested in renting a house in Franklin, he said he had only one available but would be glad to show it to me. On the way from Atlanta I had made a list of everything I wanted in a house, and this one had everything I had listed. I went back to his office and signed a contract that afternoon.

I flew home, talked to the children about it, and spent a week getting my things packed. On Saturday morning, I loaded my faithful African violet, the children, and pillows and blankets in my Ford station wagon and started out for Franklin. A moving van was to follow with our furniture.

A hundred miles outside of Tulsa, the Ford broke down. I had been telling the girls that we had nothing to fear by leaving Tulsa, that God was going to go with us and watch out for us, so now I said, "Well, girls, here's our first chance to see how God is going to help us." We prayed one of those "boy, God, do you ever have an opportunity to shine" prayers, and as soon as we had finished, a man pulled up behind us in a blue and white truck, towing a horse trailer.

He got out and walked up to our car.

"Are you ladies having trouble?" he asked.

"Well, our car just quit on us and I don't have any idea what's wrong with it or how to get it going again," I said. "If you could help us, we'd really appreciate it."

"Let me have a look under the hood," he said. "I'm no mechanic but it might be something real simple."

He worked with the car's electrical wires for a few minutes and soon the engine was humming again.

"Where are you folks headed?" he asked, brushing off my attempts to thank him.

"We're moving to Franklin, Tennessee," I answered.

"Well, what a coincidence," he said. "I live right near Franklin. Why don't you just follow me so I can be sure you don't have any more trouble?"

When retelling this incident to my friends, I've been asked whether or not this man was an angel. I don't think so, because he gave me his business card. I don't think angels carry business cards.

As we pulled back onto the highway, the girls and I laughed because God had come through with such flying colors. Not only had He fixed our car but He had sent someone to watch over us all the way to Franklin. It was practical proof that we could trust Him. From then on, we knew that God was watching over us at every point. I often told my friends that He was so much like a husband, He did everything but take out the trash.

We arrived in Franklin twenty-four hours before our furniture did, so the first night in our new home, we spread pillows and blankets on the floor in my bedroom, near the vent where the warm air came out of the furnace, and snuggled together.

The next day our neighbors from down the street, Clay and Faye Harlin, brought over a big pot of chili for us.

The Mongs, who lived behind us, came over with soup and cleaning supplies, and Ron and Patti Christian, the neighbors across the street, came up and introduced themselves. This was a far cry from living ten years behind gates with bars, TV surveillance, twenty-four-hour guards, and no neighbors, and we reveled in it. Many nights, especially in the summer, we'd sit out on the porch with our neighbors after dinner and talk while the children played in the yard. We found a little church, First Methodist of Franklin, and I began writing music again.

The girls and I also decided that every normal American family needed a dog, so we went to the pound one afternoon to find one. As soon as we saw Buffy, a tan and black-colored mongrel, huddled in the back corner of her cage, imploring us with soft brown eyes to rescue her, we knew we had found our dog. She has been a wonderful pet and this summer she had her first and last litter of puppies.

I started living in blue jeans and shorts. Gradually, my silk and satin clothes found their way to the back of the closet as the T-shirts came out. Many times my pastor would come to visit me and find me in front of the TV, ironing, clad in jeans and a T-shirt, with no makeup on and my hair pulled back in a ponytail. It was the total antithesis of the life I had lived before. I no longer had a live-in maid and nanny or four staff gardeners. Once a week I'd have a day-helper, but for the most part I did my own housework. It was during this time I also had my first experience in mowing a lawn.

One blazing summer day I borrowed Ron and Patti's mower, which, unfortunately, did not come with an instruction booklet. After I finally figured out how to operate the machine, it was high noon. Undaunted, I started out. I mowed and mowed until I thought I was going to drop. Every twenty minutes I had to stop, come in, lie down on the floor on top of the air conditioning vent, and drink iced tea. The yard was on a hill and rather than mow the logical way—horizontally—I mowed vertically. More than once I almost ran the mower into the street because I'd get it going and couldn't stop. When it reached the bottom, because of the angle of the terrain, I had to get on my hands and knees to push it back up the hill. The effort was phenomenal. It was just one of many experiences in self-sufficiency, all of which were new to me.

We stayed in that home for six months and then I bought a rambling 140-year-old Victorian house in the middle of town, where we still live. It is a wonderful barn of a house, with a cavernous kitchen and fireplaces in every room. A glassed-in sunroom runs along one side of the house and opens onto a brick patio where I've held many informal parties in the summer. The atmosphere is usually one step away from chaos, thanks largely to the activities of my children and their many little friends.

For me life has settled into a round of slumber parties, PTA meetings, ballet lessons, Thursday night prayer meetings and biweekly carpools with five eleven- and twelve-year-olds and myself stuffed into a Toyota. Sometimes I feel as if we have been enrolled in a three-year deprogramming course designed especially for us.

The past three years have been a healing and growing time for us all. I have spent many hours sorting out my feelings, repenting for my sins and failures, and seeking restoration. Franklin has been an excellent place for me to learn how to bring my ideals in line with reality (a process that seems never-ending). In confronting my own sinfulness, I have tempered the crusading zeal that caused so many problems at ORU and in my marriage.

Things no longer seem as black and white to me and I no longer feel that I have all the answers. These days I am more interested in asking the right questions—and in listening for God's answers. I have been humbled by the realization of how pathetically inadequate even our best human efforts are. I have become less eager to change the world, and more willing to allow the Father to change me.

Happily, one of the changes He has brought about in me is that I am now able to look into the mirror, fully aware of my weaknesses, and still say, "I like you, Patti Roberts. You've got some gold inside of you." That may be the clearest indication I have of God's healing power—that I can accept myself.

Another important change has involved my attitude and relationship with Richard. The events surrounding our divorce were so painful and so devastating that for many months I could not view him with anything but hatred. We communicated only when we had to make arrangements for the children, and those encounters were always tinged with bitterness and hostility. I was so absorbed in my own pain that I couldn't see Richard's pain. But, gradually, as God has healed many of my wounds, I have been able to see the hurt in Richard's life and to pray for his wholeness. My contempt for him has turned to compassion. The farther I get from the divorce the more I am able to see that there are no "good guys" or "bad guys," only wounded people in need of forgiveness and healing. I would like to be able to say that there is no longer any animosity between Richard and me, but that is not true. We still have great gaps in our communication, but for the first time in many years we are both open to the possibility of wholeness and are actively seeking it.

These past three years have brought great changes in

my girls' lives also. They are slowly adjusting to our family's new status. God has blessed us with the friendship of several wonderful married couples who have adopted us and continually watch out for us all. Russ and Tori Taff, Melvin and Edie Spain, and Milton and Nancy Geiselman cluck over my children, caring for them as if they were their own. Russ, Milton, and Melvin each bring a kind of fatherly love into the girls' lives.

For the first time, this year it was not so painful for us to celebrate Christmas as a threesome. We bought a twelve-foot-tall tree and decorated the house with joyful abandon. Christmas Eve we attended a concert that celebrated Christ's coming, and Christmas morning Melvin and Edie joined us for breakfast and gift-opening time.

In my heart and in the hearts of my children, I can see many of the old scars losing their redness and gradually fading away. I know now that there is nothing that can ever happen to any of us that God can't take and by His love cause beauty to emerge. He has made very real in our lives His promises in Isaiah 61:3. He has truly given us a "garland instead of ashes; the oil of gladness instead of mourning and the mantle of praise instead of a spirit of heaviness."

CHAPTER FIFTEEN

The True
Christian Marriage

The story that you have just read is probably disconcerting at best, enraging at worst, to many of you. Perhaps you would have chosen for me to remain silent, to not pick the scab of the memory of our marriage and our divorce.

It would be more comfortable for all of us if I had remained silent. But after our divorce, I began to notice that many of the couples around us were grappling with the same dragons. Marriage destruction is rampant within the Church. The disease does not limit itself to foot soldiers but aims with deadly accuracy at the leaders of the Body. When will it end?

Never! Unless we begin saying by our actions and prayers, "ENOUGH."

I think, in light of the many failed marriages around us, that ignorance can no longer be termed bliss. I believe that the Church must look full face at the facts and build her war strategy accordingly. Silence has been a costly luxury that we can no longer afford.

From the facts of our story as I have related them here, I hope a picture has emerged in your mind. Richard and I were two spoiled, willful, prideful people who often put our own individual happiness and devotion to the ministry above the fulfillment of our marriage vows. During much of our married life, we did not live or act as two

Christians should. I am not attempting to evade responsibility for either our sins or our failures. I think there are several important lessons that can be learned from our divorce that would apply to any Christian marriage.

First of all, marriage should be entered into soberly and only after much prayer, counseling, and genuine soul-searching. It should never be seen as a means to an end, whether that end is to escape an unpleasant family situation, to acquire financial security, or to further a ministry. Both parties need to have a clear understanding of the realities of married life. So many of our perceptions of love and marriage have been shaped by romantic films and novels that young couples are often woefully ignorant of the sacrifices and hard work involved in building an enduring relationship. Certainly Richard and I had no such understanding.

Second, the Bible makes it very clear in several places (Gen. 2:24, Matt. 19:5, and Eph. 5:31) that a prerequisite for marriage is that "a man shall leave his father and mother and shall cleave to his wife." As one preacher has paraphrased it, "without the leaving there can be no cleaving." I sincerely believe that throughout our marriage Richard never made that emotional and psychological break from his parents—particularly from his father. I don't believe he ever really established his own identity or discovered what his potential in God might be outside the Oral Roberts Association. It may very well be God's highest will for Richard to work with Oral and to become his successor. But God may have had something far different in mind for Richard. I'll always wonder what would have happened in our marriage if Richard had been able to make the parent-break.

Third, a husband and wife must make the maintenance and preservation of their marriage their first priority. Ministry cannot come before it; careers cannot come before it; even children cannot come before it. Building an enduring marriage requires a daily renewal of the commitment they first made in their marriage vows. It requires keeping short accounts with each other, not letting little irritations and hurts build into big resentments. If Richard and I had dealt constructively with the small problems in our lives, they would not have become so overwhelming.

Had we done all of these things, our marriage certainly would have had a much better chance for survival, but I believe that there were other destructive elements at work in our lives that might have caused it to fail anyway. It is these that I want to discuss briefly now, because I think those pressures are administering the final blow to the marriages of many Christian leaders today.

In the past two or three decades, the American Church has unwittingly allowed a climate to develop in which decadence is permitted and even encouraged to flourish. It has happened gradually, almost imperceptibly, but it has happened nevertheless. It reminds me of the story I heard once about a rather hideous experiment in which some frogs were placed in a bowl of water. The water was heated very gently, and by the time it was boiling, all the frogs were dead. None of them made any attempt to get out because the heating was done so gradually.

I would suggest that the Church today is like those frogs. We have allowed the pressures and the pleasures of the world to entice and entrap us until in many ways our lives are not discernibly different from those of our unbelieving neighbors.

Although this tendency manifests itself at all levels of our lives as believers, one of its most notable expressions has been the creation of a Christian subculture, or perhaps more accurately, a "superculture."

Included in this "superculture" are pastors of large,

successful churches; television and radio ministers; well-known evangelists, authors, musicians; and Christian "celebrities" of every description. They are the objects of our respect, our loyalty, and our admiration to a degree that often borders on idolatry. They are our new "would-be saints" and we have canonized them with great amounts of wealth and power, with few demands for accountability.

In this I believe we have been tragically naïve and scripturally ignorant. The Bible is full of warnings about the corrosive effects that both money and power can have on the human spirit. And while I do not wish to take an extreme position that equates poverty with spirituality, I think that many segments of the Christian community today are advocating the equally extreme but opposite position that equates success with spirituality. We need to take a hard second look at what the Gospels have to say about the uses, and abuses, of wealth and power.

Jesus dealt with both very succinctly. He never said that material success was wrong. He simply stated a fact about human nature which we seem to have forgotten: where your treasure is, there will your heart be also. It is simply impossible for a man to serve two masters; he cannot serve man and God simultaneously. If your treasure is your ministry, then inevitably you will devote your heart and all your efforts to sustaining it. And a ministry, however God-breathed its beginning, can become a substitute for God.

In his book *My Utmost for His Highest*, Oswald Chambers warns against this very thing. He says: "Beware of any work for God which enables you to avoid concentration on Him. A great many Christians worship their work or church. A worker without this solemn, dominant note of concentration on God is apt to get his work on his neck. Consequently, he becomes spent and crushed. There is no freedom, no delight in life, if nerves, mind and heart are so crushingly burdened that God's blessings cannot rest."

I would submit that many of the problems that are befalling ministries today—financial pressures, family crises—are not the result of satanic attack, as is often claimed, but the fruit of our own sinfulness, of our own divided purposes. We are attempting to serve two masters. We have put the *work* of God above God, even resorting to ungodly means to achieve our ends, and God's blessings cannot rest on us.

In many cases even our ends have become subverted. Where once our goal may have been to see the kingdom of God established on this earth, it has now become the maintenance and preservation of our "ministry." This is especially true if the ministry is successful. The accoutrements of power and wealth, combined with the continual reassurance from our adoring, uncritical public, can be a potent narcotic.

We are a nation addicted to success. The pursuit of it is our national, secular religion. And a large segment of the Christian Church appears to have acquired the seemingly insatiable hunger for that which so characterizes our culture. If you doubt that, ask yourself how many sermons, radio or television messages, cassette tapes, or books you have seen or heard lately that promise in one way or another to convey the secrets of success. Then try to remember how many you have seen or heard on the subjects of holiness, building godly character, or repentance.

Success is not intrinsically evil, but it can easily lull us into spiritual apathy and dull our senses until we no

longer hear that still, small voice with which the Holy
Spirit speaks to us. Should it then surprise us to see the
flowering of the fruits of decadence? If the Church
adopts the world's value system and the world's methods of accomplishing its ends, then it will also acquire the
world's problems.

The gospel of success and personal fulfillment at any
cost, carried to its natural extremes, inevitably leads to
the belief, expressed or not, that anything which stands
in the way of our individual happiness, be it a difficult
marriage partner or a biblical injunction which we find
onerous, may be discarded with impunity. Thus it becomes easy to justify our greed, our lust for power, and
our selfishness. And, sadly, we know that in most cases
no one will call us to account for it. There are few bold
prophets in the Church of God today. If there had been
more, Richard and I might still be married, and the character of our ministry greatly changed. Perhaps our priorities would have been restructured to align with the
Word of God.

At this point, I want to emphasize, however, that the
Roberts family is not unique in this respect. For every
excess or abuse you have read about here, dozens worse
could be cited. Every vice of the secular world—drug and
alcohol abuse, immorality, child abuse, sexual perver-
sion, mismanagement of funds—can be found in the
Christian "superculture." And the people involved are
not evil people. For the most part they are sincere Christians whose ministries were originally based on a genuine call of God. But somewhere along the way they lost
their perspective, and what was begun in the Spirit is
now too often maintained in the flesh. And a segment of
the Body of Christ, intoxicated with its newly acquired
respectability, continues to applaud. As long as these
individuals are able to maintain the dashing good looks

of success, few look beneath the high-gloss performance to see if there is any substance behind the glitter.

A good example of just how far we have come in this direction was provided by Jerry Falwell during the last presidential election. Falwell was caught lying about, or at least misrepresenting the truth about, a conversation he supposedly had with Jimmy Carter at the White House over the issue of homosexuality. When Carter produced tapes of the meeting which exposed the deception, Falwell's response, as quoted in *Newsweek* magazine was that the incident was "unfortunate," but all that pastors really had to worry about was making sure that they were not caught in adultery or stealing funds from the church.

This illustration is not used to condemn Jerry Falwell; I believe he is a godly man who simply got carried away in the heat of his political rhetoric. What I find significant is that he could make such a statement about morality and that it, along with the original deception, could go unchallenged by the religious community. Surely we have not yet reduced the Ten Commandments to two?

If some of you think I am making a mountain of a small molehill in this instance, perhaps you're right. But I think it is indicative of a general malaise that is spreading rapidly through the Body. When ministers know that they can divorce and remarry almost at will; when Christian musicians learn that as long as they keep producing hit records they can lead decadent personal lives; when Christian publishers of magazines, music, educational materials, and books are allowed to employ questionable business practices as long as the bottom line remains healthy; and when the Church requires of its leaders no other accountability than the accountability of success, corruption is inevitable.

Until the Church is willing to give up its idolatry, to

prefer purity over popularity and power, then it will continue to be plagued by problems. There will be more broken homes, more shattered ministries. The cartoon character Pogo summed up our position succinctly when he said, "We have met the enemy and he is us." I believe that the biggest threat to the Church today is not from Satan or the world, but from ourselves.

"Help us! Help us! We're under Satanic attack!" is currently a voguish kind of plea from various television ministries. To be sure, those that are building God's Kingdom on this satanically occupied territory will always be under attack of some sort. After all, we are at war. But we, as the informed Church, must also consider: Are the attacks outgrowths of our own stupidly greedy decisions toward indulgence? Are they products of our own poor planning? Or are they a full frontal offensive from hell? We can quell some of this activity merely by making Spirit-led decisions rather than decisions led by the flesh in the conduct of our corporate as well as individual ministries. And rather than blast those who differ with us, let us remove from our collective camps the evidence of self-willed decisions. That having been done, our efforts in battle will have a more authentic tone to them.

It is time for us who are the Church to grow up, to repent of our sin and reassess our goals—both corporately and individually. In our reassessment, however, we must be careful to avoid the sin of judgment. The Church must not abet Satan and heap criticism on those who have failed. Condemnation is a cheap thrill once repentance has occurred, and who among us is big enough to question the efficacy of the blood? The true test for us as believers is—can we love and embrace those who are scarred by failure and thus cause the Church to become stronger at the very point at which Satan intended that she be destroyed? I believe we can. Even as we look honestly at failure, at sin, at human weakness, we the Church, must still become Christ's instrument of redemption to ourselves and to the world.

That will only occur as we submit ourselves, individually and corporately, to the wishes and ways of God—no matter how high the cost—and as we enter into deep, sustained prayer.

If you have been disturbed by some of the revelations in this book, I plead with you, do not condemn any of its principals. View our failings in the light of Galatians 6:1: "Dear brothers, if a Christian is overcome by some sin, you who are godly should gently and humbly help him back onto the right path, remembering that next time it might be one of you who is in the wrong." Before hurling judgments at us, examine your own hearts. Ask whether, under the circumstances, you could have done any better or even as well. Do not forget or negate the truly wonderful accomplishments of Oral Roberts simply because he is human, with human weaknesses. Pray for the entire family.

Finally, I would call you to pray for the Church.

The destiny of the Church is so glorious and so power-ful as she stands poised at the edge of eternity, waiting to step into her role as Christ's spotless bride. But even as we rejoice in that prospect, we also at times despair as we look around us. Certainly the Church today is far from spotless. It is torn by doctrinal battles, bloated by excess, horrified by the failures of its leaders, and often clearly defiant of Christ's laws of love. Often the religious super-structures on which we hang our religious activities seem to have little to do with the true Church of Jesus Christ.

We may wonder how such a group of fragmented, war-torn soldiers can cross the bridge from here to eternity.

We start out with thanksgiving because we know that Christ has promised the Father that He will complete the process begun at Calvary. He will cleanse us and make us ready to assume our eternal role. The purification process has already begun. Much of what we attribute to Satan today is, I believe, the merciful judgment of God, the discipline of a loving Father.

But it's time for us as individuals and as a Church to say to the Father, "Wash me, fill me with Christ's love for You, for myself and for this tired world with its unholy ways of doing things. Cause to grow in me a protective love and respect for the other members of Your Body. Grant to all of us the courage to seek the truth in our actions and a resolve that when the truth is revealed we will not recoil in horror. Instead, cause us to war in prayer for healing and wholeness wherever we see sickness and weakness.

"Give us the power to take the stones we wish to hurl at those who frighten us or disagree with us or injure us, and instead build an altar with them. Give us the courage to mount that altar and say, 'Here I am—make me into Your image. Let me decrease in fame and power as You increase in glory and might.' Hasten the time that we should be transformed into the bride."

> Shrouded in sorrow, sometimes dressed in shame,
> Through the ages she stood it all for the honor of
>   His name.
> There were times she watched her children perish
>   in the martyr's flames,
> While remembering that purity is sometimes won
>   through pain

Slowly she shakes herself as His strength pours
    through her veins.
And He whispers, "I've trained you well, now the
    time has come to reign.
So arise, dress in royal robes, prepare yourself for
    Me.
Come, My bride, come, My love, let's share the day
    of victory."
Here He comes, the King of glory,
Coming for His bride.
And she rises to meet Him through the fire
    purified.
Oh, Church, the day is coming,
Perhaps, the day is here, when the skies will break
    open and Jesus will appear.*

Patti Roberts has always been a familiar voice in gospel music with her records, TV appearances, and concerts. And after a long period of silence Patti has a new desire in her heart. With it comes a fresh selection of songs that convey some of her deepest thoughts and convictions. They have all been captured on her recent Word album, WINTER TO SPRING (WSB-8893), available at your local Christian book/music store.

Patti Roberts
P.O. Box 1129
Franklin, TN 37064